SMUGGLERS' TALES

SMUGGLERS' TALES

TOM QUINN

DAVID & CHARLES

PICTURE ACKNOWLEDGEMENTS

The author and publishers would like to thank the following for their help in supplying illustrations for this book. Every effort has been made to trace copyright holders; we apologise if any have inadvertently been omitted.

The Bridgeman Art Library/ p1 Chris Beetles Ltd., London, UK, p2 (Atkinson Art Gallery, Southport, Lancashire, UK), p36 (Victoria & Albert Museum, London, UK), p79 (Bonhams, London, UK), pp100–1 (Victoria Art Gallery, Bath and North East Somerset Council), pp134–5 (British Museum, London, UK), p153 (British Museum, London, UK), p171 (Private Collection), p175 *Lynmouth, Devon, the Story of the Shipwreck* by Albert Goodwin (Maidstone Museum & Art Gallery, Kent, UK), p186 (Musée de la Chartreuse, Douai, France/Giraudon); Cecil Aldin, pp3, 7, 9, 15, 45, 104, 141, 161, 177, 191; Fred Roe, pp5, 14, 103, 129, 130, 173; Sotheby's, pp8, 10–11, 115; The Sutcliffe Gallery, pp12–13, 41, 94–5, 138–9, 185; National Trust Photographic Library/Mike Williams, pp18, /Rob Matheson, 66, 151, /Graeme Norways, 108-9, /David Sellman, 119, /Joe Cornish, 147, /Ian West, 159; Derek Croucher, pp24–5; *The Countryman*/John Edenbrow, pp33, /Edwin Smith, 38–9, /John Saunders, 55, /F. Shuter, 77, /J. Allen Cash, 112, /Dennis Mansell, 127, /Derek Widdicombe, 180; Mary Evans Picture Library, pp35, 49, 51, 59, 61, 71, 87, 93, 97, 107, 178, 188; Paul Hardy, pp43, 105, 155, 157, 163, 169; Museum of London, p80; from *Smuggling in Sussex* (Wm Cooper, 1858), p90; Beverley Richardson, p143; from *Smuggling* (Hyatt Verril), p165; J.B. Pyne, p187.

(Page 1) Smuggler's Cove, *an illustration by Rowland Emett for* Punch, *1942*

(Page 2) The S̶ .... t Gallery, Southport)

(Page 7) *Locals face the wall so as not to see the smugglers*
(Illustration by Cecil Aldin in Smugglers' Gallows*)*

A DAVID & CHARLES BOOK

First published in the UK in 1999
Reprinted 2002

Copyright © Tom Quinn 1999

Tom Quinn has asserted his right to be identified as author of this work in accordance with the Copyright, Designs and Patents Act, 1988.

A catalogue record for this book is available from the British Library.

ISBN 0 7153 0696 0

Printed in the UK by Butler & Tanner Limited, Frome
for David & Charles
Brunel House   Newton Abbot   Devon

Fred Roe.

CONTENTS

FOR EMMA

Thanks to all those authors, living and dead, whose work I have consulted. I'm grateful
to Sue Viccars at David & Charles and to Julia Hiles and Kate Spiers at
The Countryman magazine.
Many people contacted me by telephone and by letter while I carried out the research for
this book, and although I have not been able to follow up every lead, I would like to
express my thanks to R.T.F. Burrows, Barbara Doyle and the staff at the British Library.

The Smugglers' Song

If you wake at midnight and hear a horse's feet,
Don't go drawing back the blind, or looking in the street;
Them that ask no questions isn't told a lie,
Watch the wall, my darling, while the gentlemen go by.

Five and twenty ponies
Trotting through the dark –
Brandy for the parson
'Baccy for the clerk;
Laces for a Lady; Letters for a spy;
And watch the wall, my darling, while the gentlemen go by.

RUDYARD KIPLING

THE SMUGGLERS *by George Morland*

INTRODUCTION

To this day beneath many old inns and houses along almost every stretch of coast from Land's End to John O'Groats there are deep cellars and passageways which once provided a secure store for smugglers' contraband. Some pubs had hidey-holes behind panelling or under floorboards, or holes dug beneath grandfather clock cases so that bottles could quickly be disposed of. Other houses and barns on lonely headlands can still be seen with their curious tiny windows built high up in the eaves; here the smugglers' lookouts sat patiently to signal with an old horn lamp when the coast was clear.

Smuggling has a rich history, for it was part of the fabric of all our lives – even those of us whose ancestors lived inland – for many centuries: indeed, until the middle decades of the nineteenth century, smuggling was an almost universal activity throughout Britain. The smugglers themselves, far from being reviled as criminals, were celebrated as local heroes. They were genuine Robin Hood figures who, if they didn't quite take from the rich and give to the poor, at least made sure that all but the very poor could afford luxuries that would otherwise have been the exclusive preserve of the rich.

Smuggling wasn't just something that involved the poor and ill educated, either: it was not uncommon for the local gentry to be involved; parish priests almost invariably turned a blind eye to the trade in return for the odd keg of brandy; and there are many instances of local magistrates either helping the smugglers or at least ignoring what they got up to. Even the excisemen – known also as blockademen, customs men and searchers – frequently took part in the smuggling and then informed on themselves, or more precisely on the contraband, which as part of an elaborate ruse they proceeded to 'seize'. As a result they earned a reward which was of more value in most instances than the smuggled goods.

Why was this? Well, the reason has a great deal to do with the simple fact that government taxes on imports and exports of a great variety of goods were ill thought out, often excessive and invariably impossible to enforce. High taxes ensured that the vast bulk of the population would never be able to afford to drink wine or spirits or tea, or to wear silk or smoke tobacco; at one stage even salt was taxed heavily. Taxes that created this situation were bound to be ignored, particularly in an island nation noted for its seafaring skills. For an experienced skipper, the short journey across the Channel or over to the Dutch ports

where prices were unimaginably lower was all in a day's work – such a trip would bring pleasure to the smuggler's home village and profit to himself. It was irresistible, and the increasing severity of the law had, by and large, no effect since informers could rarely be found, witnesses always turned out to have noticed nothing, and juries to a man refused to convict.

So exasperated did the authorities become that they offered huge rewards to anyone who would inform against the smugglers. However, despite the large sums offered, these rewards were only rarely successful, for the truth is that among village communities local loyalties ran deeper than money could fathom, besides which, anyone who took the money and informed on the smugglers knew that at best they faced ostracism, and at worst death.

The smuggling era in Britain has its origins in the vast wealth created by the wool trade in the late Middle Ages. When wool exports began to be taxed heavily, wool began to be smuggled – something that was easy in an age of remote communities and no effective customs service. Centuries later customs men were employed everywhere, but still they could do little to stop the smugglers.

By the mid-eighteenth century a vast range of what we would now term luxury imported goods were being heavily taxed: the list included silk, tobacco, tea, rum, brandy, whisky. Poverty caused by falling agricultural prices in the late eighteenth and early nineteenth centuries exacerbated the situation, as did the return of large numbers of discharged soldiers and sailors after the end of the Napoleonic wars. Despite having served their country, often at the cost of a leg or an arm,

Smugglers' den: taken by Frank Meadow Sutcliffe, this is probably the only photograph of genuine smugglers in existence

these men were left to fend entirely for themselves. Inevitably many turned to smuggling.

Inevitably, too, given the universality of smuggling and the glamour of the smuggler's life, legends and stories grew up about the battles between smugglers and the excisemen, and about the extraordinary antics of charismatic individual smugglers. Of course, there are also many tales of brutality, for there is no doubt that when cornered the smuggler could be a very nasty customer indeed; there are many instances of battles between the authorities and smugglers' bands that left men seriously injured or even dead. In the main, however, smuggling stories – whether from the highlands of Scotland, the wide sands of East Anglia or the rugged coats of Cornwall and Devon – are stories of what one might best term 'honest roguery'. They are classic stories of secrecy, daring and adventure.

An old time 'lookout', West Mersea

This book draws together a vast number of the best of these stories, many of which are long forgotten or have never been told before. They come from the personal memories of families whose ancestors were smugglers, from dusty record offices up and down the land, and from old, long-forgotten books and vanished newspapers and journals. It is extraordinary that our huge store of smuggling stories has so rarely been explored. Certainly smuggling inspired a vast amount of fiction in the late nineteenth century when, of course, the glory days of the smugglers were still well within living memory; but little has been done recently to collect the far more enthralling flesh-and-blood stories. I hope and believe this book fills that gap.

ROGUES' GALLERY

Smuggling legends and stories handed down from generation to generation in most parts of Britain include a fair sprinkling of extraordinary characters whose lives and exploits ensured their permanent place in smuggling history. Some of these characters were out-and-out villains, others were hard men who showed only an occasional hint of generosity or compassion, while one or two seem almost to have been gentlemen first and smuggling rogues second – which may explain why they occasionally risked being caught in order to help a friend in need or even to help an exciseman down on his luck.

More typical is the smuggler with a sense of humour or mischief, who enjoyed teasing the government-employed exciseman to whom he invariably felt superior both intellectually and as navigator and seaman. Two examples of the crafty smuggler – the cool customer who enjoys teasing his adversary and sees attack and bravado as the best form of defence – were recorded by the Victorian writer Athol Forbes:

BLOOMIN' CHEEK

'A daring piece of coolness took place at Hartlepool. A fish salesman, Horsley, was augmenting his income by a little smuggling. A consignment arrived earlier than he anticipated. The Dutchman's vessel stood into the bay and began making signals and his mission about as public as it could be under the circumstances. But Horsley had a fine nerve, and he went to the coastguard station: "I want protection," he said to the chief officer. " That Dutchman is bringing over some bulbs for me, but he is a madman, the skipper, and to tell you the truth, I am afraid of him when he is in drink."

'"I'll send a couple of men with you," said the obliging officer.

'"I think if you send the coastguard pinnace, it would give the bully a fright that would last him all his life," said Horsley. "There's no doing with these Dutchmen," he continued. "They think themselves superior to an Englishman." "Oh, do they," snapped the indignant representative of the Service.

'"Man the pinnace," he called out to a subordinate. They rowed off to the Dutchman. Horsley climbed on board and got an opportunity of instructing the skipper in his part. The pinnace stood by.

' "He won't let me bring my bulbs away, and I have paid him the money," Horsley shouted to the boat. The Dutchman appeared at the same time, gesticulating wildly. Two coastguards were ordered on board, and the chief officer accompanied them.

' "Which are your cases?" they asked. They were pointed out. "Have you been paid?" The skipper sullenly replied that he had. "Very well, what more do you want ? Get those cases into the pinnace."

'The Dutchmen, thoroughly cowed, or pretending to be, did as they were directed by the man in blue and gold, and in a few minutes Horsley and his contraband were being rowed ashore in comfort and safety by Her Majesty's servants. What is more, the coast-guards helped to get the packages into Horsley's warehouse in the town. Of course, the chief officer found out eventually how he had been hoaxed, but the only wise course for his own sake was to keep silence and make no charge or complaint.'

CAUGHT RED-HANDED

On another occasion the writer's grandfather, a customs man, told him the story of a smuggler who, being caught red-handed, brazened his way out of an extraordinarily tight corner. Mr Forbes again takes up the story, which comes from what was still the coast of Northumberland, before local government reorganisation:

'A fisherman was steering his coble into the mouth of the river Tees, and decided to land at a place called Seaton Snook. It was a fine evening, and he ran his coble upon the beach. His boy called his attention to a man seated among the long grass skirting the sands. Here was an awkward predicament, for no doubt he was a patrol. But the fisherman was equal to it. He waded ashore and walked up to the concealed man.

' "I want your help," he said. "My coble has a plank that's lifted. Do you mind helping me to drag her up the beach?"

'The man addressed pleaded his duty and the want of a pair of seaboots. Mending cobles and wading after them was not his routine. Besides, the tide was running out, and the coble would be high and dry in a few minutes. The fisherman sighed, and said he supposed he would have to wait.

' "Here, boy!" he shouted. "Leave the coble and run up to the farm yonder for a hammer and a few copper nails."

'The boy ran off to the farm and waited a goodly length of time, and when the coast was clear and the patrolman had gone, he brought a man and a couple of pack horses. Later on the coastguardsman had a painful interview with his chief, and there was more than the usual amount of merriment in a score of houses and inns of that neighbourhood.'

However, despite occasional lapses like this, the excisemen were no fools and in many areas they built up elaborate networks of informers of varying degrees of reliability. But the success of a customs raid or the veracity of an informer's piece of information had to be treated with caution or the whole thing could turn into a disaster, both for smuggler and exciseman, as the historian Hyatt Verril recalled in 1924:

A dog turnspit in a kitchen at Newcastle Emlyn, South Wales by Thomas Rowlandson c1800

'Copping kept his promise and turned in the contraband in the hope of being pardoned. He led the officers to the brandy casks, but he had failed to mention that they were quite empty. He also failed to mention that he had hidden a bundle of smuggled silk into the first hiding place at home that came to mind – the oven.

'When the customs men saw that the kegs were empty they were furious, but they could do nothing and the smuggler returned to his home. But the joke was on him, because in her hurry and confusion, his wife had forgotten that the oven was heated for baking, and the precious smuggled silks were done to a turn!'

A CERTAIN CODE OF ETHICS

Talk of honour among thieves may be misplaced, but it is difficult to discount one or two smuggling stories that indicate a strong code of ethics – of a sort – among those who engaged in the running trade. One member at least of the Carter family, notorious for generations in their native Cornwall, illustrates the point. Hyatt Verril tells the tale:

'One of the most famous of the smugglers' resorts was a spot known as Prussia Cove on whose shores dwelt the Carter family, famous as smugglers. On one occasion, when the elder Carter was absent, the officials raided the spot, found a quantity of brandy, and confiscated it, placing it among other seized contraband in the government warehouse.

'When Carter returned he was furious, not that he resented the excise officers taking the brandy so much as the fact that, as he put it, he would be unable to deliver the spirits to his customers and they would think him dishonest and unreliable. Quite wrought up

over the matter, he determined to raid the warehouse and recover his brandy, which he did, meticulously removing only his own casks. When day dawned and the outrage was discovered, the officers instantly averred that Carter was the culprit, and when asked why they were so sure, they declared that "No one else would be so honest as to take only that which belonged to him!"'

The Tale Of Peter Trent

Without question the most remarkable tale of a smuggler prepared to rise above petty considerations of traditional enmity is that of Peter Trent who risked his life to save the crew of a boat sent to arrest him. The tale is told by a number of nineteenth-century authors, but what follows is the gist of it.

He was, so the story goes, headed across the Channel one stormy night towards the end of the eighteenth century – for like other smugglers, he would always choose the worst possible weather for running contraband – when, as he neared a remote cove on the Cornish coast, a flash of vivid lightning revealed a vessel in distress to the east. What she was or who were her company, Peter never stopped to question, because by the intermittent glare of the lightning he could see she was in dire straits. One mast had already gone, her sails had been torn away, and she was driving helplessly toward the rocky cliffs looming faintly above the gleam of white water at their feet. It was an all but crazy undertaking for Peter to attempt to run alongside and rescue the men: a wave might drive his boat against the other and smash her; both craft might be in the breakers before he could transfer the crew of the other to his own vessel; and even if he succeeded in doing this without mishap, it would be ten chances to one that he could not work off the lea shore in the gale and turmoil of the sea. But Peter never hesitated to go to her aid.

Mutiny Aboard Peter's Boat

His men, however, became almost mutinous. It was all very well to save a fellow mariner in distress, but what, they argued, was to be gained by adding their own lives to those about to be sacrificed? And as they neared the other craft and recognized her, they flatly refused to obey orders. She was a revenue cutter, and while they, like their fellow Cornishmen, had no desire to murder a revenue officer in cold blood, neither had they any intention of risking their own lives for the sake of saving their enemies', only to be arrested by the rescued men.

In vain Peter argued, threatened, pleaded. And then, finding the men would go no farther, and being obsessed with the idea that by his superior skill and knowledge of the coast he might yet save the cutter, Peter stripped off his Guernsey and before his men could stop him, leaped into the raging sea. As if by a miracle, he managed to reach the tossing, reeling, unmanageable craft safely, and clambered aboard.

Smugglers' bay on the rugged Cornish coast: a perfect spot to land a cargo of contraband

Peter Is Too Late

But he had risked his life in vain, because he had arrived too late to prevent the cutter from dashing itself to destruction: hardly had he gained the decks when she struck. With a sickening crash, the jagged rocks tore through her hull; her remaining mast was flung like a javelin over the bows, and then, on a following sea, she was lifted, hurled forward and left – crushed, battered, a mass of wreckage – upon the narrow strip of shingle at the base of the cliffs. In another moment a breaker would come roaring in, and there was no time to lose and only one small chance of saving their lives: shouting to the panic-stricken men, Peter leaped ashore and began climbing like a cat up the cliffside, followed by the others. Before they had gained a yard, a wave thundered about their feet, drenching them with spray, almost tearing them from where they clung. Then as the wave rolled back, they worked their way inch by inch higher up the sheer wall of rock.

A few feet above the hissing, thundering seas they reached a narrow shelf of rock and could go no farther. Above them the rocks leaned outward, smooth and unscaleable. Exhausted, shaking, drenched, they clung to the narrow ledge, shivering and numbed with the cold, biting wind. And then a new and even more fearful terror seized them: the tide was rising, and already the sea covered the shingle, already the spray was dashing itself about their feet. Far away Peter's lugger was working off shore; no help could come from that direction. Above them the cliff vanished in the blackness; below them the relentless tide was rising, inch by inch, inexorable as fate. Soon the incoming waves would drag them down to death – and rather than face being drowned by inches, rather than endure the torments of watching the inexorably approaching hungry waves, one man threw himself into the sea. The others declared their intention of following: they gripped hands, and were on the point of casting themselves from the ledge, when a glad shout from Peter stopped them.

Peter Perceives Some Samphire

'We're safe!' he bellowed, making his words heard above the screech of wind and roar of surf. 'Safe!'

Before their wondering, uncomprehending eyes he held out a tiny bit of green, a tender sprig he had plucked from a crevice of the rock whereon he clung. 'The tide will never reach here,' he cried, seeing the men could not grasp the meaning of his words. 'It's samphire !'

Then, at last, they understood. They all knew that the little plant never grew below high-water mark. The tiny spray of green, and Peter's knowledge that it was samphire, had saved them, and with renewed hope they clung to the rock. Up the cliff side the waves crept; a few inches beneath the ledge the breakers hurled themselves and boiled in fury – and then slowly, imperceptibly, the waves receded, the tide went down, and as day dawned, gray and sullen over the channel, the strip of shingle was once more revealed, with a narrow, rock-strewn gulley leading from it to the summit of the cliff. But Peter was nowhere to be seen. In the black night, as the men had watched with straining eyes fixed upon the ever-rising sea, he had vanished. None doubted that, unseen and unnoticed, he had dropped into the sea, and sorrowfully, fully realising that they owed their lives to his bravery, the men toiled up the tortuous way and gained the uplands.

However, Peter had not met such an untimely fate as they supposed. He had found a tiny cleft in the rock wall and had crept stealthily along it, and had then made his way in some incredible manner to the summit of the cliff; and as the rescued officers gazed seaward, they saw Peter's lugger putting to sea, with the unmistakable figure of Peter himself at the helm!

SMUGGLING'S PRACTICAL JOKERS: NEVILLE OF GUERNSEY

As well as acts of extraordinary bravery, smuggling seems to have generated a huge number of practical jokes – the smugglers, it seems, were not content merely to outwit the revenue men, they also wanted the revenue men to know they had been outwitted, and one sure way to do this was to set up elaborate plans of deception or to organise practical jokes. This brings us to the notorious Neville of Guernsey, who was, if numerous early authors are to be believed, noted more for his sense of humour than for his courage or smuggling deeds. He dearly loved a practical joke, and especially if the joke was on the revenue officers. On one occasion, while in an alehouse, he heard a trio of customs men discussing means of reaching an out-of-the-way spot where, so they had reasons to suspect, a cargo of contraband was to be landed.

Here was an opportunity exactly to Neville's taste. Approaching the officers he confessed to overhearing their words, and declared he knew the coast well; he then proposed that he would be only too glad to carry them to the desired spot in his boat, and would like nothing better than 'to put them after the smugglers.'

Never suspecting that the man was a notorious smuggler himself, the officers gladly

Taproom of a Country Inn, from a sketch by Thomas Silson, 1837

accepted his offer, and a little later embarked in his vessel for the secret cove. It was only a short run, a matter of a few hours, but the officers, knowing nothing of the coast and still less about boats, were not in the least suspicious when Neville headed for the open channel.

Hour after hour passed, and the officers began to grow impatient and demanded why they were taking so long. Neville offered some unintelligible explanation regarding currents and winds, but assured them he would put them ashore in a few minutes. And he kept his word to the letter: running into a little cove, he saw his passengers disembark, and immediately sailed away. Plain upon the sand were the imprints of the feet of many men leading inland – but even the excise officers could see that the smugglers had come and gone, and angrily they turned to berate Neville. But he was already well out from shore. Gaily waving his hand, he shouted farewell, and added, 'I kept my promise. I put you after the smugglers – four hours after them!'

Of course, the craftiest smugglers knew that putting the stuff ashore was only half the battle – the real test was conveying it to a place of safety away from the ever-prying eyes of the revenue men and their spies. Many smugglers went to great lengths to cover their tracks, and they usually maintained a network of 'safe' houses whose architecture was frequently adapted to the needs of concealing large quantities of contraband. However, these safe houses could bring trouble on their otherwise innocent occupants. A.K. Hamilton Jenkin, an indefatigable collector of smuggling stories from the West Country, is the main source for the following story.

A Narrow Escape For Trevaskis

During the earlier half of the nineteenth century a smuggler called Trevaskis lived in west Cornwall. He had acquired more than a local reputation for his success in running goods upon the coast, and in finding safe hiding-places for them afterwards till the danger of discovery was past. It so happened that on one occasion a cargo was expected in a little cove to the west of St Ives, a secluded spot admirably suited for the smuggler's needs. Among the few inhabitants of the valley was the owner of a grist mill, a simple old fellow who had never had any dealings with the smugglers himself, but who, on being approached by Trevaskis, good-naturedly gave permission for the storage of some of the goods on his property.

This was done, and all seemed well until a few weeks later when a party of excisemen arrived one day at the cove. They immediately began poking about the place, and in so doing discovered a nest of brandy-kegs cunningly concealed in one of the old man's furze ricks. The miller, needless to say, was terribly upset, dreading the loss of his reputation as an honest man even more than the legal consequences of his complicity. At length, however, in return for a bribe of £200 which comprised his life's savings, he succeeded in persuading the king's officer to hush the matter up.

It would appear, however, that in the course of the inquiry the miller must have revealed the part which Trevaskis had had in the business, for shortly afterwards the sarcher – the exciseman – hoping no doubt for another fat reward if he succeeded in catching so notorious a smuggler, called on the former and charged him with what he knew.

The smuggler, being of a very different type from his confederate, told the exciseman bluntly that he 'warn't going to pay no bribe', and that 'they could put him up to Bodmin (the assize town) if they'd a mind to.' To Bodmin, accordingly, he had to go, accompanied by the exciseman, who no doubt felt in high spirits. At Hayle the couple boarded the train at the little station which may still be seen in Foundry Square, beneath the arches of the more modern railway line. Passing along under Clifton Terrace and through the grounds of the present Penmare House, the train at length reached the foot of Steamer's Hill, near Angarrack, where a stationary engine at that time pulled the trucks up a steep incline to a point near the present Gwinear Road station. On this occasion, however, the train had not got more than half-way up the incline when the wire rope attached to the front carriage parted. Back rushed the trucks gathering terrible speed, till finally, reaching the bottom, they crashed into a bank and overturned.

Strange to relate, few of the passengers were seriously hurt and only one was killed, that one being the exciseman! With no one who could now act as a witness against him, Trevaskis took his own release and returned home, amidst universal triumph, to his own village.

THE QUICK-WITTED TAILOR

Luck, of course, was only one factor in the smuggling game; even more important was quickness of wit. Another Cornish story, this time of a certain quaint old journeyman tailor, Lewis Grenfell, illustrates the point.

One cold mid-winter day, Grenfell and a companion were removing a cask of brandy from one of the mine tunnels which formed a favourite hiding place for smuggled goods in this district. They had just brought out the cask from the tunnel in question when, as luck would have it, an exciseman was seen approaching.

The tailor's companion, thinking discretion the better part of valour, promptly took to flight and hid himself in a thick furze brake near at hand, leaving the other man to face the situation as best he could. In answer to the officer's stern inquiries, Grenfell, who appeared to be shaking with the cold, admitted his offence – indeed, with the incriminating cask beside him he could not do otherwise – but pleaded in extenuation his extreme poverty and the needs of a large family and a sick wife. Finding, however, that pathos produced no effect upon the exciseman, the old man begged only that he might be allowed to taste a drop of the precious liquor to warm his shivering bones.

To this the officer agreed, and handed him a gimlet with which to make a hole in the cask. The tailor's hands were numb, however, and his movements so slow that at length the exciseman, who was also quite ready for a drink, leapt down from his horse and, handing the reins to Grenfell, began opening the cask himself. Hardly had he begun to do so, when the tailor, perceiving his chance, jumped onto the horse's back and made off at a gallop.

The officer thereupon gave chase, and scarcely were both men out of sight round the shoulder of the hill, when the tailor's companion crept out from his hiding-place and quickly secured the cask – which, needless to say, the exciseman never saw again!

Wild Cornish coastline at Kynance Cove

An Audacious Swop

Spirits, of course, were not the only form of contraband handled by smugglers, as the following story reveals. Again it comes from a number of sources, and is also a wonderful example of the audacity of individual smugglers.

One day, a man named George Michell drove up at the door of the Angel Hotel at Helston, Cornwall, in a spring cart, the back portion of which was closely covered with a sheet of tarpaulin.

'What 'ave 'ee got in there?' inquired the landlady, coming to the door to meet him. 'Silk, my dear,' replied the man. 'Do 'ee want to buy some?'

'Hush,' replied the landlady,' I thought as much, and what's more there is others know of it. There's a party of sarchers in the bar waiting for you now. They'll be out any minute. What are 'ee going to do?'

Without a word the man jumped down from his cart, and throwing the reins to his son, bade him drive into the inn yard. Proceeding himself towards the bar, he greeted the excisemen with a friendly nod.

'A cold day, gentlemen,' he remarked. 'What about a drink all round?' The excisemen, having their man in sight, willingly agreed.

'I expect you found the wind pretty cold crossing Goonhilly Downs this morning,' said the officer with a knowing glance; 'you come from St Keverne, I believe. Do you know if there's been much smuggling out that way lately?'

'Aw, ais, pretty fair, I believe,' replied the other, 'and there would be plenty more if you chaps wasn't always so darned smart. No good for the poor smugglers to try and deceive you. You can see through their tricks every time. It beats me how you do knaw so much.'

An innocent-looking waggon is checked at a tollgate

Between drinking and chatting, the man contrived to spin out a considerable time. Suddenly, however, there was a rumble of cart-wheels and the sound of horse-hoofs outside. One of the men rushed to the window, in time to see an old-fashioned box-hearse being driven out of the inn yard.

'Only a pauper's funeral,' he remarked, as he rejoined the others by the fire. They finished their glasses, and then the officer rose and, putting on an official air, turned to the other and said, 'George Michell, for that, I believe, is your name, I have a warrant here to search you and the cart in which you drove up just now. I must ask you to accompany me into the yard.'

Nothing loathe, the other led the way. The tarpaulin was removed, only to disclose to the sarcher's gaze the usual market produce – several baskets of eggs, a few fowls, and some butter.

'Is that all, friends?' inquired the owner, 'because if so, I must be going about my business – and you, I expect, have yours!'

TALES OF WOMEN SMUGGLERS

Tales of women smugglers are very rare, but one or two have come down to us, and perhaps the most surprising thing about them is how fierce these women were. One suspects that in an age when any kind of an active working life was difficult for women, a smuggler woman had to be ten times as fierce as her male counterpart just to survive. Various writers and historians have told the tale over the years.

Bessie Catchpole

After the battle of Waterloo, many battleships returned to the work of preventing smuggling; it was a time when the coastguard had most of the advantages over the smuggler. However, despite the difficulties, Bessie Catchpole became notorious among the smugglers and excisemen of the east and south coasts. Her address was a changing one, sometimes Harwich, at other times Ipswich. Her husband had been killed in an unsuccessful running of tobacco and brandy, and Bessie took over her husband's interests. At times she dressed as a man, smoked a pipe, and wore a formidable cutlass, and when, on the occasion of his death, she appeared so arrayed on the deck of her husband's yawl, the *Sally*, the men, sullen with defeat and loss, brightened up at once and gave her a ringing cheer. In a few words she announced that she was the new skipper, and that the business would be continued under her directions. A Dutchman who gave a loud guffaw and remarked upon her attire, she promptly knocked down with a blow from her fist. This appears to have been the first and only attempt at anything approaching insubordination. Nothing succeeds like success, and for some two years or more she continued to make successful and profitable runs.

Ashore, Bessie was held in the greatest respect by clergy and gentry, and Sunday she invariably kept as a day of rest; what is more, she made those under her respect its sacred character. Every voyage witnessed some new ruse on her part. Returning from Dunkirk on one occasion, she hoisted a yellow pocket handkerchief (yellow was a signal that the ship's crew were sick) at her mizzen. Cutters and men-of-war swarmed in the Channel, but Bessie Catchpole steered straight for a King's ship. Suddenly the gun-brig went about, and stood away to the north: they had caught sight of the yellow signal, which meant plague, and they preferred other work of a more healthy character. No doubt her boldness in steering straight for the King's ship helped make the impression upon its officers that she wanted medical assistance, and as they were in the vicinity of the coast, the captain naturally thought there were more medical men ashore, and better qualified, for such work. So, unmolested, Bessie landed her cargo not far from Ipswich.

On another occasion she was closely pressed by a cutter. The wind fell, and both ships lay becalmed, and night came and hid the one from the other. Bessie put out all lights, but

Rigging out a Smuggler, by T. Rowlandson

in the darkness the kegs of brandy were got out, lashed together like a string of beads, floats fixed, and the whole arrangement put overboard. The kegs were then sunk, and Bessie had them moored with grapplings; the only signs were an empty fish trunk or two.

With the first suspicion of dawn came a boat fully manned from the cutter. They had been out all night looking for Bessie, and the officer and men were in an ill humour. They swarmed over the side, and were met by the apparition of Bessie, who welcomed them cordially. Yes, she was Bessie Catchpole, she replied to the lieutenant's question, and this was the smuggling yawl *Sally*, and she had no objection to them searching her vessel. This was already being done, but nothing was found of a dutiable character. The officer was furious.

'Why did you run away from us last night?' he demanded.

'Had I known you were on board and coming to see me, I would have waited,' she said, and the crew laughed. 'But some of you King's men have very naughty characters, and I wished to protect myself,' she added. Her banter was more than the disappointed officer could stand, and refusing her invitation to breakfast, he ordered his men into the boat and cast off.

It was, of course, quite an easy matter for Bessie and her crew to pick up, later in the day, her cargo left in the care of Father Neptune; and again a successful run stood to Bessie's credit.

Cunning Old Age

When it came to smuggling, neither age nor sex was a bar to success. Youngsters barely out of school were among the most audacious and energetic smugglers – and for slyness and cunning, old age could actually be an asset, as the following tale, culled from a number of Victorian sources, reveals:

An elderly lady wearing blue spectacles was a regular passenger on the Ostend boat. She claimed her only object in crossing was to convert the wicked foreign people from the error of their ways, and for this purpose she was armed with a plentiful supply of religious tracts printed in English. These she distributed to passengers, and she instantly befriended any clergy who might be on board. However, one day the customs officers took it upon themselves to examine a parcel of her tracts lying done up in the ordinary bundles among the luggage; and sure enough, although there was a tract pasted on the outside, the inside consisted of excisable goods.

She must have defrauded the revenue out of thousands, for her trade had been regular over many years, most people having a deference for an elderly lady engaged in religious work.

A Gloved Hand

A clever deception, again carried out by a woman, was played upon the revenue when a duty was exacted upon imported gloves. The French make were in great demand, and customs began to make seizures of large cases of these luxuries; however, upon examination it was found that all the gloves were for one hand – there was not a single pair. All seized

SQUIRE JIM AND WILLIAM ON LONDON BRIDGE,
EIGHTY YEARS AGO

goods were sold, but odd gloves were no use and there was only one bid at the auction, from a lady. As a result they were knocked down at a ridiculously low figure.

Some time afterwards two revenue collectors were talking over customs matters when one remarked upon the frequent seizures of gloves in his port. The other had the same experience to tell, and he, too, told of the lady who bought up the goods afterwards. Comparing notes, it was found that the lady was identified with the purchase of gloves at the London Custom House, and at Bristol and other places.

If a thousand gloves for the right hand were smuggled and stopped in London, a thousand corresponding ones for the left hand were imported through Bristol. The lady bought both lots at a low figure, and then she had complete pairs. It was estimated that she had defrauded the Revenue out of some thousands of pounds, at little trouble and comparatively no risk. She retired from the business before she could be located and caught. In London alone her business showed enormous profit.

Jack's Swimming Adventure

John Banks, a notable mid-Victorian historian of smuggling, wrote and published his account called 'Jack's Swimming Adventure' in 1871. Like a number of other authors who recorded the story, he was clearly impressed by the resourcefulness of its hero, a local man always likely to get the better of his adversaries – who were probably outsiders anyway. The story starts at Pier Rocks, the name once given by residents of Hastings to the remains of the old pier which, at the time Banks was writing, could be seen at low or even half tide.

A lugger had been despatched to France for goods, and it was pre-arranged that she should arrive off the Pier Rocks on a certain night. On that day Sam, a sort of foreman in the matter, said to Jack, a fellow-workman and one of the company who were to smuggle the goods, 'Jack! do ye mind going off in a boat to-night?'

'No,' said Jack.

'Can ye swim?' asked Sam. Jack answered yes, and it is arranged that they will go at a certain hour. Sam, as we have said, was in charge, and this meant he had his work cut out for him because in the early part of the nineteenth century the customs men had honed their skills. The smugglers therefore had to be supremely well organised in order to escape detection.

Sam and Jack set off at the time appointed, Jack dressed so as to be able to swim easily with his clothes on. They went quietly out in their boat until they fell in with the lugger carrying the goods; the lugger got in as near as she could approach with safety on a pitch-dark night. The tubs of spirits, being already slung in pairs, were attached to a long line and without a sound were put overboard. Jack, with two of the crew, proceeded quietly in their little boat towards the shore, towing the tubs behind them.

Suddenly they saw another boat coming towards them and, thinking it was a coast-guard boat, they assumed the game was up. However, it turned out to be the crew of a Deal lugger, which was simply lying nearby.

They rowed in slowly to the back of the Pier Rocks, and noticed as they went the lights from vessels unloading in the fishmarket. Jack now slipped overboard with one end of the line round his body, and telling his companions to be sure to give him enough slack, he cautiously swam in westward of the Pier Rocks. The others in the boat, getting clear of the line, made their way towards the shore, eastward of the Pier Rocks, to deceive (if necessary) the coastguardsman, should one be stationed at that particular spot, and draw his attention from Jack and his transactions.

Jack quietly swimming in, sees the dark outline of the Pier Rocks against the somewhat lighter sky, and after a minute or two, fancies the rocks are in motion. It's the men from the smuggling lugger who have managed to get there, and they are waiting for him.

'Is that you, Jack?' says one, in a quiet voice. 'Yes,' says Jack, 'it's me.'

'You can land there, I think; give us your line.'

The goods are soon hauled silently in, and as silently are distributed, the company making their way along some sand which had been deliberately sprinkled across the beach; and as it happened on this particular night, the coastguardsman on duty at the western end of the Parade was held in conversation by someone (a tradesman) who was 'in' on the secret. The company and goods were soon away.

They went up into Hastings, into West Street, through Russell Court, along George Street, up the Light Steps, and along Hill Street. In this street they saw a light – old So-and-So was not gone to bed: it being Saturday he was having a hand of cards with a friend. A smuggler went in and borrowed the key of the card-player's shop; the goods were stowed away in the shop till the next night, and then, all being quiet, they were taken to their destination and nobody the wiser – the transactors excepted.

The irony of all this was that Jack's father was a custom-house officer, and on this particular night had been performing his duties as coal-measurer on board one of the vessels that was unloading opposite the fishmarket. His duties over, he had gone to Jack's lodgings, and was having a wash before going to his home at Guestling. Jack was in a dilemma, as he dared not go in wearing his wet clothes, for fear of betraying the transaction in which he had been engaged; he was therefore obliged to have recourse to the good offices of a neighbour, who smuggled to him a dry suit of clothes, in which he was able to put in an appearance as a dutiful son.

A Lucky Rabbiting Outing

Jack seems to have been a lucky rogue as well as a crafty one. The story is told of how he and a friend were fortunate enough once to stumble - quite by chance - across five tubs of spirits which had been hidden on a cliff-top. They were strolling along the top of the East Cliff just outside Hastings one afternoon in the 1820s, hoping to pick up a rabbit or two, having a ferret and a dog with them. The previous day Jack had been assisting his father at the Custom's warehouse, and his long blue frock had a whisky scent about it. Whittaker, Jack's friend, kept on sniffing and said he was sure he could smell spirits; Jack told him it

High seas over Sheringham, Norfolk: it was the smugglers' mastery of the seas that kept them one step ahead of the revenue men

was his frock, and explained the cause. 'No, no,' said Whittaker, 'it's too strong for that.'

Looking about they saw a mark where a rock had been cut by a rope, and they knew at once that some goods had been hauled up the cliff during the previous night. They managed to descend onto a ledge a little way down, and there, to their surprise, they found five tubs of spirits. They very quickly took them away to a cottage near the Rocklands, and were paid six shillings per tub by the owner. Not a bad afternoon's work!

But the risks of smuggling soon grew too great even for Jack – this was, after all, right at the end of the great days of smuggling – and soon after he got married, gave up smuggling and disappeared from history.

THE CIVIL SMUGGLER

What Jack achieved by cunning and daring, other smugglers sometimes achieved by politeness and civility, whatever the provocation. This probably had a great deal to do with the laws of navigation and seamanship which were almost always strictly adhered to both by smugglers and customs men; but for one or two individual smugglers, civility was a sort of trademark. Jemmy Roper, another Hastings smuggler, is a classic example. John Banks, that indefatigable chronicler of all things to do with Hastings, actually met him, as he recalls:

'It was the custom at the turn of the nineteenth century for people connected with the contraband trade to assemble in small parties of ten or twelve on the east and west hills on a summer's evening for the purpose of regaling themselves with a glass of spirits and a quiet pipe. So common was this practice that it was thought nothing of by people in general. Indeed, the merchants on the other side of the Channel not infrequently threw in an extra half-keg of spirits for the express purpose. Townspeople passing for a walk were, if known, invited to take a glass, as was indeed once the case when my father, after his day's work, was about taking his boys for a stroll in the fields.

'A frequent guest at the little hillside parties was a fat, good-natured fellow named Roper, who commanded a remarkably lucky, fast-sailing lugger called the *Little Ann*. So far from assailing the excisemen with taunts and abuse, like the rest of his comrades, Roper conducted himself with undeviating civility; so that had it been possible for fire and water to unite, he would have been esteemed even by his opponents. He usually wore a long white frock or gabardine over his everyday clothes, and it was his custom, when not engaged in illicit adventure or enjoying a cliff-top party, to sit smoking his pipe and swinging his legs on an old seat fixed in the beach in front of the Cutter public-house. He was often asked why he did not quit smuggling altogether and turn fisherman? This was one the few things that seemed to make him irascible.

'"What? Would you have me sit bobbing an eel all day to catch sixpenn'orth of whiting? No; I was born a smuggler, I was bred a smuggler, and I shall die a smuggler – but I have no wish to see my children tread in the same footsteps. If either of my boys gets into a boat, I'll either break his legs or make him a linendraper sooner than he shall learn all the trouble his father has experienced."'

Signalling to the smugglers' ship

35

Snatched From The Jaws Of Defeat

All smugglers were to some extent at the mercy of chance and good or bad luck, but few can have been quite as fortunate as Joe, a late eighteenth-century smuggler who, after a potentially disastrous mishap, managed to snatch victory from the jaws of defeat. Again, John Banks is the main source for the story:

'Joe was once taken up by a group of excisemen as he was going with his horse and cart to assist in a smuggling transaction. The excisemen, who had already seized some smuggled goods, told him, in the king's name, that it was his duty to assist them in conveying the goods to the custom-house at Hastings. Of course, Joe could not help himself. It was early morning, and the place near Great Worsham Farm, at Bexhill. The excisemen loaded Joe's cart with twenty-three tubs of spirits, one quarter keg, and two bags of tea. Some of the batsmen – smugglers armed with sticks and clubs to fend off attacks – who had been engaged in the night's smuggling transaction, had managed, after the goods had been seized,

The Smugglers by William Barnes Wollen

to make a circuit round nearly to the spot where they were being loaded in Joe's cart. At or near the spot there was a slight bend in the road, and Joe caught sight of one of the batsmen looking round the bend in the hedge; rightly surmising that he was not alone, he signalled for him to come on.

'A body of batsmen immediately rushed round the corner, and drove off the excisemen. Joe applied his whip to his horse, drove off at full speed, and did not draw rein till he reached Sedlescomb, where there was another horse and cart in waiting, in which the goods were safely carried to Rye. Joe was paid seven pounds for this smart bit of work, and was kept at Sedlescomb, living in clover, for a week.'

The Story Of A Suffolk Shepherd

Perhaps more realistic than many accounts of swashbuckling smugglers who fought terrifying battles regularly on the high seas, is the following account of a Suffolk shepherd who smuggled, as so many did, in his spare time. The story was first published by that great recorder of rural life George Ewart Evans, and comes from a 1950s edition of that splendid magazine *The Countryman*. It was written by the Victorian naturalist G.T. Rope, although it was not published in his lifetime. Rope's manuscript is still owned by descendants of the shepherd described.

Liney Riches, or Richardson, was a highly skilled and well liked shepherd. He and his family lived in a remote cottage on the heath near Blaxhall. In his spare time he grew splendid vegetables and fruit in his cottage garden; he was famous for his skill at growing greengages. Much of his time was spent with his flock on the heath round about – a pond at which he regularly watered them is still referred to as Liney's Drink and an ancient burial mound of the sort common in many parts of England, much frequented by Liney, is still known as Liney's Mount.

Liney was of about middle height. He had good, regular and rather refined features. His gait, like that of many whose work is entirely restricted to the tending of sheep, was quite free from the swaying rolling movements so often acquired by those who have long been accustomed to follow the plough. With his shepherd's slop or smock flowing gracefully behind him, with crook on shoulder and dog at heel, he would sail grandly along behind his sheep at a steady even pace, his body leaning slightly forward and head thrown rather back; a picturesque figure in the landscape and a personage of importance – the man to be consulted in all cases of illness or injury to sheep.

He had the courteous and respectful but dignified manner often noticeable in the older shepherds and farm labourers of his time. His greeting was usually, 'Sarvent, sir,' or 'Sarvice tie yor, sir'. His speech, hardly intelligible to one unfamiliar with the pure Suffolk dialect, was rather slow, deliberate and free from all hesitation or uncertainty.

Liney was a skilful trainer and handler of a sheepdog, and almost always managed to have a good one. His old yellow-and-white Bob used to go about in summer with his head and ears bound up in a crimson handkerchief as a protection from the flies. He was one of

the first in his district to make use of Scotch dogs for his work.

Liney's life appears to have followed the usual course for a farm worker of that period: long hours, a large family and almost constant poverty, if not actual want. But there were ways of relieving this, and the more enterprising men in the district were not slow to take advantage of them. Liney worked at a farm not two miles from a narrow inlet on the coast, and along with a number of other local men, was hand-in-glove with smugglers. Cargoes of contraband were landed regularly at the small inlet and dispersed overnight. It was not unusual for a farmer to hear two or three of his horses being taken out of their stables, and he was discreet enough to turn over on his pillow and go to sleep, knowing that the horses would be back in their stalls in the morning. They might have a bit of sweat on them perhaps, and not too much zip in them for the next day's ploughing, but the farmer knew that he would be well compensated by finding a barrel of wine or spirits hidden in the corner of the barn under a pile of straw.

On these nights Liney Richardson's job was to turn out his flock of sheep and follow the waggon closely to the place where the contraband was to be loaded. He was careful to get his sheep to walk directly behind the wagon, right over the tracks, especially on the return journey, and it was an astute customs man who could find a trace of waggon wheels after Liney's sheep had been walking the road. In spite of this, the risks were great and the penalty for smuggling, even as late as the mid-nineteenth century, very severe. When Liney was out with the smugglers, his wife used to gather the children round her and sit in front of the fire with the cottage in darkness. The children knew that they dared not breathe a word until their father had returned and their mother was free from the agonising suspense.

A lonely Suffolk farmhouse – an ideal hiding place for smugglers' booty

When one tries to picture him on Liney's Mount it is hard to dissociate the shepherd of tradition, standing there watching his sheep, from the man preoccupied with other problems: how many sheep he could safely take with him down to the cliff that night, and how he could pick out a score or so of quiet ones. In fact the noise made by these as they were being driven probably went unnoticed, for within living memory there were numerous breeding flocks in the parish with a total of not less than two thousand ewes.

The two aspects of Liney Richardson's life were symbolised by his dress. He wore a smock made from eight yards of drabbet – that is, drab, twilled linen. It was beautifully honeycombed across the chest and shoulders; there were no openings front or back, and the garment was warm and almost weatherproof. Inside it were two long hanging pockets, and a couple of rabbits or a brace of pheasants could easily be concealed in its folds.

THE SMUGGLER'S WIFE

The one person almost invariably braver and more resourceful than a smuggler was a smuggler's wife. The following is a classic example of the terrors occasionally inspired by the distaff side:

A man once called upon the preventive officer at an east coast port and gave valuable information which led to the capture of a cargo of tobacco and spirits, and eleven or twelve smugglers. The informer asked for no reward and refused it when offered. Questioned as to his motive, the officer elicited the information that the skipper of the captured lugger had mercilessly flogged the man's son, the flogging being for the purpose of procuring a change of wind. The mother of the boy threatened to inform of this attempt to smuggle and to give other information besides, unless her husband turned king's evidence. He evidently preferred the terrors of the smuggling fraternity to the vengeance of his wife.

BESSIE MILLIE, THE WITCH

We turn now to the curious figure of Bessie Millie who, strictly speaking, wasn't a smuggler at all. However, with her local reputation for unearthly powers she was an enormous asset to the Orkney smugglers, who no doubt paid generously for her help. The story was originally recorded by Athol Forbes in his book, *The Romance of Smuggling* published in 1909:

'At the village of Stromness, on the main island of the Orkney group, lived a witch called Bessie Millie who, for well on into the nineteenth century, gained a living by selling favourable winds to mariners, and providing luck charms for the whalers. Her power and influence were paramount in that part of the Northern Islands.

'At that time the captain of the Revenue cutter HMS *Widgeon* – my grandfather – was ordered to hunt out the smugglers and put down their traffic with a firm hand. He was chosen for this post for his intelligence and for signal gallantry.

'From the first he found himself thwarted and baffled by the witch Bessie Millie. Soon after his arrival my grandfather was surprised to find her standing before him in his cabin.

A wonderful photograph from late-nineteenth century Whitby, a town with a long tradition of smuggling

He sternly demanded from the sentry why the woman had been allowed to invade his sanctum unannounced. The man, a brave and splendid seaman, said she had threatened to blind him and he believed she could do it. He ordered the man under arrest and the woman to leave the ship.

'"Not before I have had my say," she said. "George Phillips, you come from a proud, wilful race, and most of yer brood have met death by sword, bullet, and violence; beware how ye defy Bessie Millie."

'My grandfather had all the old-world notions of chivalry in regard to a woman, even if she were a witch. He hesitated about laying hands on her. She stood before him habited in a loose hand-woven gown, a plaid shawl of some tartan about her shoulders, and a handkerchief round her head. Her face presented all the appearance of discoloured parchment, her dark eyes were deep set, and flashing with fire. A massive masculine brow and a firm jaw completed her description. "Say what you have to say and be gone," said he, not knowing what else to do under the circumstances.

'With an utterance of astonishing rapidity and a wonderful choice of words she enumerated certain events in our family history, particularly in connection with the disastrous uprising in favour of the Stewarts in 1745. That my grandfather always maintained she must have learnt from local history, but what did astonish him was her knowledge of certain facts which he did not know then, and which eventually turned out to be true. The object of her visit was no doubt to frighten him, and intimidate the crew so that their vigilance on behalf of her smuggling friends might be interrupted by fears of her vengeance.

'When she directed my grandfather to take his ship back to the cursed government that had sent him he laughed. With the crew she was more successful.

'A report was brought that a cargo was to be landed in one of the numerous creeks on the main island. A couple of pinnaces were sent off to watch the inlet, while the cutter stood out to sea to cut off any escape that way, should the men get away from the preventive guard. To the amazement of my grandfather the two pinnaces returned to the ship within a couple of hours and the officer in charge reported a mutiny.

'While proceeding up the inlet Bessie Millie had appeared on the headland and ordered the men back to the ship, threatening them with curses when they hesitated. What is more, several of the men took to their hammocks and declared they had been bewitched, and discipline was for a time at an end. Calling together what men he could rely on, my grandfather sought the witch. Her house was situated on the brow of the hill overlooking Stromness. She was on the threshold awaiting them, a look of triumph on her face. "George Phillips, I told ye that ye would come to me before I would come to you."

'"Well, I have come," was his reply, "and unless you come down to the Widgeon and remove your spell, I will burn down this haunt of yours." He had to proceed to put this threat into execution before she consented. The men who said they were sick quickly recovered, and something like an armed truce prevailed between the Government ship and Bessie Millie. But she always seemed able to divine the plans of my grandfather, and on more than one occasion she was the means of frustrating them.'

A PACT WITH THE DEVIL

For out-and-out style, few smugglers can compete with Yawkins, the terror of eighteenth-century Northumberland customs men, and a smuggler whose story must have enlivened countless convivial evenings down the years. Yawkins was notorious on the coast, of Northumberland and the Scots coast right up to Edinburgh, and just his name struck fear into the hearts of the officers of the Revenue.

He made the most of the fears that his presence inspired on one celebrated occasion when, happening to be ashore with a considerable quantity of goods in his sole custody that had paid the king nothing in the nature of taxes, a strong party of excisemen bore down upon him. Instead of bolting in the face of superior force, he sprang upon them shouting: 'Yawkins is before you! Come on, my lads!' The revenue officers were so intimidated that they relinquished their spoil, and the men took to their heels.

On another occasion Yawkins was landing his cargo at the Mankman's Lake, near Kircudbright, when two revenue cutters, the *Pigmy* and the *Dwarf*, simultaneously hove in sight on different tacks, the one coming round by the Isles of Fleet, the other between the Point of Rueberry and the Muckle Ron. The dauntless free-trader instantly weighed anchor and bore down right between the luggers, so close that he tossed his hat on the deck of one and his wig on that of the other, hoisted a cask to his maintop to show his occupation, and bore away under an extraordinary pressure of sail without receiving injury. To account for this, and other hair-breadth escapes, popular tradition alleged that Yawkins insured himself against capture by a bargain with the Evil One, this being that the devil should have one-tenth of his crew each voyage.

His vessel, famous for many a day, was the *Black Prince*. She used to discharge her cargo at Luce, Belcarry, and elsewhere along the coast, sometimes running as far down as the Tyne and the Tees.

· A LANDING AT BO-PEEP.

The Last Of The Cut-And-Thrust Smugglers

Our final loveable rogue comes from Essex, that low-lying county of marsh and inlet whose smuggling history has never been fully explored. Old Pettifer, who is mentioned in a number of old books, was most lovingly recalled by Fred Roe in his book *Essex Survivals*, published in 1929:

'In my youth I conversed freely with a very ancient specimen of the old-time cut-and-thrust smuggler – almost the last of his race – a gnarled mariner who admitted that he had cheerfully proposed to drown in deep water a couple of intrepid coast-guardsmen who boarded his lugger. Discipline and the strong arm of the law prevailed against his lukewarm backers, and my aged acquaintance, a likely young fellow then, got a term of what he was wont to call "King's Pleasure". (This happened, he explained, in the last year of William IV.) In a more than usually strenuous struggle, one of his eyes was knocked out, and it was with a solitary orb that the ancient reprobate eventually used to sit, discussing hot rum, with a superannuated customs officer in the latter part of his life. The hatchet was quite buried those days, and the two members of opposing factions were often to be found hob-nobbing in front of the fireplace of the "Ship Ahoy".

'Old Pettifer (his name was not quite Pettifer) is gone, many years ago now, but I remember as yesterday his knotted veinous hands as he rowed along in his rotten tub of a boat, and the fire that shot out of his lone orb as he described his capture when his mates hung back cowed. "They fellows," he vociferated, "hadn't no pluck or we'd been clear of Brass Buttons."

'I have scant sympathy with contraband traffic, but as I recollect old Pettifer he was very honest, and desperately poor. A Suffolk man by birth, I believe, but his great and happy hunting ground – to use a poor metaphor – was the Stour rather than the Orwell. Toward the end of his life he earned a scanty living by vending hat-guards; for the crazy boat in which he once rowed out confiding pleasure-seekers went to pieces some years before its master. His age was phenomenal, and he could only be coaxed to talk with difficulty, but when wound up it was not easy to stop him. And his language when I – engrossed in his yarns – managed to steer his craft head-on to a floating buoy, was marvellous to hear.'

CUTTERS & LUGGERS

Throughout the long history of smuggling, the two sides – smugglers and excisemen – wrestled for mastery of the seas. As the smugglers made their boats faster, the excisemen responded in kind: it was a bit like Russia and America during the Cold War, when each side strove ceaselessly to develop weapons and equipment that would be faster, more accurate and more deadly than those developed by the other side. In the case of the smugglers the important thing was to have the best boat and the best skipper, because that way you could almost always outrun the enemy. The excisemen knew this was the smugglers' game, however, and they responded by employing the best boat-builders that money could buy – and with the backing of government money they often did have the edge, at least in theory. In practice, of course, the skill and daring of individual skippers would often ensure that the smugglers' vessel escaped even the best government boat.

Battles on the high seas were therefore commonplace; but in their zeal, the excisemen sometimes made mistakes, as the following story reveals. It comes to us, via a number of sources, from the coast of East Anglia.

THE BOMBARDMENT OF DUNWICH

One night as the villagers of Dunwich slept peacefully in their beds, their village, situated right on the coast, was apparently attacked from the seaward side. There were the cannon balls – but somewhat baffling was the fact that they were of British make, hall-marked, genuine articles: and yes, that *was* the mark of the naval stores. An inquiry was therefore promised.

This was a decided victory for the fathers of the village: their mayor had brought the Admiralty to book, and the logs of all the King's ships anywhere near Dunwich on that particular day were examined, or ordered to be. But strange to say, not one contained any report, or even a note relating to the bombardment of Dunwich. The matter is still receiving the attention of the Lords of the Admiralty.

What happened was this. The frigate was chasing a smuggler, which cunningly ran for shallow water. The crew of the larger vessel, seeing their prey escaping, pelted her with round shot, and as a final salute, probably fired a broadside into the darkness on the chance of hitting her. Then the sudden appearance of lights in the village alerted them to the fact that its inhabitants were receiving the brunt of the volley meant for the smugglers. Seeing that such a dire mistake had been made, the King's ship withdrew – and naturally the captain did not wish to perpetuate in his written records such an exploit; nevertheless, the 'regrettable incident' had not been invented.

Many accounts of cutters chasing luggers are tales of extraordinary skill and daring – indeed they are frequently pitched at such a level of drama that they read like fiction. One of the best examples of this kind of thing – and a story that has many of the hallmarks of telling, re-telling and embellishment – comes from the east coast, and principally from the pen of Athol Forbes.

BATTLE WITH A DUTCHMAN

The story is of the gruesome, dogged battle fought between the revenue cutter *Spitfire* and the *Hans Vort*, a Dutch lugger mounting fourteen guns and commanded by a splendid seaman, van Brunn. The *Hans Vort* used to run her cargoes into Lynn, Hull, Yarmouth and various ports on the east coast. For years she had done a roaring business quite unmolested, for there were clever minds directing all her operations; for instance, if the loading were to be done at Hull, it was intimated to the authorities that it was to be Ipswich. For three years the revenue cutter's men played a losing game of hide-and-seek, so much so that the government began to suspect that their officer was in league with the smugglers, and he was replaced.

The new officer in command was named Phillips, a young man of eighteen years of age, and naturally he was anxious to capture the smuggler at the earliest date. To his great delight he received information that the *Hans Vort* would make her next attempt to land her stuff on the Suffolk coast, and Gorleston was named as the likely place. Whether the intelligence was given by a traitor or by van Brunn, who knew of his superiority in gunpower and felt safe, will never be known. Phillips regarded the information as genuine, and kept a sharp look-out.

Sure enough, on the date named – an afternoon in late autumn – the Dutchman was seen making his way into the Yarmouth Roads. The revenue cutter's men had disguised their vessel by colouring the sails, and to dispel any idea as to their true character, Phillips manoeuvred his command in a slipshod, slovenly way, to give the impression that it was an ordinary vessel engaged in fishing. To his joy and great surprise, van Brunn came on straight for his destination, running right into the jaws of the revenue cutter.

Suddenly the Dutchman put up his helm and fired a broadside as the ship rounded, and at once it became apparent to Phillips that he was in deep trouble: several shots struck his vessel, and a large portion of his bulwark was torn away. The secret was out, loose ropes were tightened, and the revenue cutter was sailed for all she was worth. Phillips kept the wind, and his distance, and poured in one broadside after another – but he carried only four inadequate brass cannon, 'brass barkers' they were called, and their shots carried about half

The smuggler tacked between the rocks leaving the revenue craft baffled

the distance their opponents did. Therefore all that van Brunn had to do was to keep his position, use his guns, and victory was his. The result was not long manifesting itself, and by sunset the little *Spitfire* was drifting, a helpless wreck, to leeward. All her standing rigging had been shot away, and only the stumps of her two masts showed; out of thirty men, five were dead, and nearly all were wounded. The feelings of the young lieutenant may be imagined, in this, his first command, his first battle and defeat.

Sorrowfully he gave orders to drop anchor to keep the cutter from drifting ashore, and he helped to plug the shot-holes to prevent her sinking. Once the sun had set, no lights were permitted, and darkness saved them from total destruction. Nevertheless, Phillips took the bearings of his antagonist, because he had fixed upon a plan; and when he mentioned it, his desperate crew responded with a cheer. The two pinnaces were hastily examined and made watertight; every available man was then ordered into the boats, and a whipcord was run from one to the other to keep them together in the darkness; giving out a length of a hundred fathoms, the rope was also to serve them in netting the Dutchman in the dark. Phillips insisted upon his men resting for a couple of hours, then a tot of rum was served to each, and the gallant men set out.

Luck, which had deserted them, now favoured them. Before they were aware of it in the thick darkness, their rope had caught the ship they sought. Most of the smugglers were asleep, but as they scrambled up the sides a Dutchman fired a cannon into the pinnace under the port quarter, which immediately sank; but the occupants had all secured their hold on the chain plates, or had swung themselves on deck. Here a fierce hand-to-hand fight raged, and all the pent-up bitterness of those hours when, helpless, the Dutchman had mercilessly bombarded them, gave the servicemen a new strength for the fight. The Dutch, at first taken by surprise and losing heavily, soon, under the encouraging example of their skipper, pulled themselves together and fought well.

The decks grew slippery with blood, but Phillips and his men had accounted for some twenty of the smugglers on their first onslaught, and his men had been taught their cutlass drill thoroughly. It was evident that the Dutchman was beaten unless something unforeseen occurred, and van Brunn saw this. He and Phillips were now fighting hand to hand, for the Dutchman had soon singled him out. Each was a fair swordsman and a big, powerful fellow – but suddenly the sword flew out of the hand of the skipper, and Phillips immediately called upon him to surrender. But instead, van Brunn, armed only with his fists, rushed upon his adversary, who straightaway lunged at him and ran him through the shoulder – but this did not stop van Brunn lifting the lieutenant clean off his feet, and with a desperate throw the two went overboard, the Dutchman still holding on to his man. In the water Phillips killed him.

The engagement by day was watched by a crowd of people, who lined the cliff between Gorleston and Corton. They saw the revenue cutter beaten, and rejoiced, and in the morning they saw it being towed away by the lugger – that was all right, but why should the Dutchman leave without landing his cargo? Signals were exchanged between the dragoons, who had come down to the coast, and the ships – and then a cry of anger went up from thousands of throats when they found that during the night the revenue cutter's men had captured their friends.

The Capture Of The Four Brothers

A similar account, from the south coast this time, comes at first hand from one of the men involved; since few such testimonies survive, this tale is consequently all the more interesting. It is taken largely from an account published in the mid-nineteenth century under the title *Reminiscences of Old Folkestone Smugglers*, and concerns the capture of the lugger *The Four Brothers* by the revenue cutter *Badger*, after fierce resistance on the part of the crew of the lugger. This event caused a great sensation throughout Great Britain at the time, and undoubtedly inspired many of the stories about sea-fights with smugglers which came from the pens of novel writers. When the battle occurred, in January 1828, the smuggler who related what follows was in his twenty-third year; when he told his story to the historian who wrote it down, he was in his eightieth year. Nevertheless his recollection of the event was singularly clear, even to the most minute details of the fight and the subsequent events:

The sumgglers are surprised by the revenue men

'I was born in 1808, and went to sea when I was about eighteen years old, in fishing boats. When about twenty, I joined a crew of smugglers, which brought much better pay. We had a guinea a week standing money, and for every successful voyage we had ten guineas. I had made several trips from Folkestone to the coast of Ireland without meeting with any remarkable adventure. We never had much difficulty in running our cargos ashore, and then Irish people very quickly got it out of the way. Our lugger was a smart craft, and very fast; she had been a privateer, but was captured by an English vessel and sold at Southampton. An old Folkestoner bought her, and making some alterations, fitted her out for smuggling. She was manned principally by Folkestone men, and my uncle had command of her, the crew numbering in all twenty-six.

'On the 12 January 1828 we sailed from Flushing, with a cargo of leaf tobacco, upwards of a hundred tons, in half bales of 60lb besides a few kegs of brandy, and I have heard that ship and cargo were valued at more than £10,000. It used to be the practice to have whole bales, but these were unwieldy, and so they were made up specially in smaller bundles.

'A very light wind was blowing; we had got a new mainmast, and were only about half rigged, so that we sailed slowly. Just before daylight on the 18th we were abreast of Dieppe. It was intensely dark, and suddenly we found ourselves close to what we supposed were French fishing vessels. Without any suspicion of danger we held on our course, when suddenly one of the cutters, which we then knew was a revenue cutter, ran up her flag, and fired a gun to bring us to. We felt that we were in for it, but our captain determined to make every effort to beat the cutter off, and get away – and in truth, if our rigging had been complete we should have had no difficulty, but the cutter outsailed us.

'We tacked, and the cutter did the same, and firing was kept up on both sides. We carried four guns, but the cutter had more, and they were bigger than ours, which of course gave her a great advantage. As soon as all the firing began, we hoisted Dutch colours, and the fight was kept up, as far as I can remember, for a couple of hours. The fierceness of the battle may be gathered from the fact that out of our crew of twenty-six, four were killed and six wounded; how many of the *Badger*'s crew were hit, I cannot tell, but one was killed. To avoid our fire they kept below, but all our men were obliged to be on deck to work the vessel. But from the first we had no chance, and presently the cutter drove her bowsprit through our mainsail, effectually barring our escape.

'We determined to fight to the last, and to sink our vessel rather than be taken, for we knew what the consequences would be. While the two vessels were thus in contact, we thought the day had turned in our favour. Our biggest gun almost touched the cutter's bows, and we attempted to fire it. I have never known why it was, but all our efforts were unavailing, and the piece would not go off, or the cutter's bows must have been blown in. Seeing the critical position of his ship, the commander of the cutter called out to us to surrender, and promised that we should have our boats, and clothing, and go on shore.

'He was an English officer, and we trusted to his honour, but the mean hound was playing us a trick. We packed all our clothing, got into our boats with our bags, and rowed away, sorrowfully leaving behind one of our comrades, dead. But when about a quarter of a mile away, the cutter's boats came after us to force us to return. We knew then what was meant, for without arms, what could we do against two boats full of armed men? Sadly enough, we rowed back again, and for more than an hour we parleyed with the cutter's officers. It was no good, however, and we were at last compelled to go on board.

'Our lugger was taken into Dover Harbour, and the poor fellow who was killed was buried in the churchyard there. We had a sorry time of it for some days. The cutter put us aboard of the *Severn* man-of-war, where three others of our crew died, and the rest were kept in irons in the cockpit, the cold all the time being intense. After some days the cutter took us off again, and carried us up the Thames, where we were confined on the Tower tender for three or four days, and then, handcuffed and chained in an old barge, taken ashore, and lodged in the King's Bench prison. Next day we were all taken to Bow Street, and admitted for trial for wilful murder, but before our trial we laid for eleven weeks in the King's Bench.'

Chasing the smugglers…the revenue men always had a sneaking admiration for the seafaring skills of their sworn enemies

Imprisonment And Trial

The old smuggler said they were treated well by their gaolers. They were aware from the first that the defence would be based on the assumption that they were Dutchmen, and so they were warned to speak as little English as possible, which injunction they carried out. They were all confined in one ward, and allowed to have what they chose in the way of food, and the governor of the gaol had a pew constructed in the chapel adjoining his own for their accommodation. Nothing was allowed to be cooked, however, in the ward, and the old man related with great glee how on one occasion a leg of pork had been frizzled before a fierce fire by their friends outside to give it the appearance of being cooked, and was then stowed away to be properly finished on Sunday. But while it was roasting, the chief warder paid them a visit, and they were sadly afraid their savoury joint would be seized; their uniform good behaviour, however, saved their dinner. In fact they seem to have been allowed to do pretty much as they liked, prison discipline not being then so rigidly enforced as it is now.

Another remarkable incident, which the old man quite failed to account for, was this: during their long stay in the prison, they had never seen a single rat, although the place was known to be swarming, and the massive door, studded with iron bolts, left a space of two or three inches at the bottom. But during the last night of their stay, the smugglers were infested with rats to such an extent that they were obliged to leave their beds to protect themselves. Naturally enough the superstitious among them took this visit of the rats as an ill omen. But to finish the story:

On Friday the 25 April, the twenty-two prisoners were arraigned before Lord Stowell (chief judge of the High Court of Admiralty), Mr Justice Park, and Mr Baron Hullock. In the words of the old man: 'The Court was packed so full that there wasn't room to move. The dock wouldn't near hold us, so some had seats along the front outside and we took turns at sitting. They didn't try us for murder, as it was expected they would, all our friends being afraid we should be hanged, but they tried us for firing at a King's ship. We had two of the best men in England to defend us, Mr Brougham and Mr Lushington and our solicitor told us beforehand they were sure of winning. Of course there was lying on both sides; there was a great number of witnesses, and the trial lasted two whole days.'

Acquittal

'At six o'clock on Saturday evening we were discharged, the jury having decided that most of the crew were Dutchmen; if we hadn't been turned into Dutchmen we should all have been hanged, but they couldn't hang one and not the others. There was tremendous cheering and excitement when we got into the street. The first thing to be done then was to get the news home to Folkestone; accordingly a mounted messenger was engaged, and riding hard all the way, he reached here about one o'clock in the morning. Next day (Sunday) we all started for Folkestone, some by the Dover and the others by the Folkestone coach. People knew what time to expect us, and when we got to Sandgate it seemed as though all

Folkestone had turned out to meet us. The church bells were rung, I have heard, but cannot say whether it was so, our heads being completely turned at our reception.

'I never went smuggling again after that. My father took the lugger out of Dover harbour, and sailed her back to Flushing; the cutter *Badger* had to escort her, and thousands of people were present to see them depart. What became of the cargo I can't say, but it may have been carried safely to Ireland after all.'

SMUGGLERS' BOATS

The usual smuggling route from the south coast towns was across the Channel to the French ports, as one resident of Hastings, the writer John Banks, remembered in 1871. He also recalled some of the names used for smugglers' boats; for instance in the early 1800s, he tells us, the smugglers used long, fast sailing luggers which were sometimes called hackboats, sometimes constitution boats. 'I have seen them put off from Hastings, when I was a boy, it being no secret where they were going, and on what errand.' The same writer remembered the fate of one hard-pressed smuggler:

'It was often the lot of the smugglers when at sea to be chased by men-of-war. Of course the passage to France and back was not without risk, particularly when the boat was loaded with goods intended to be run. During the last century, cutters were mostly used in this business; generally speaking, they were fast sailers and could easily elude pursuit unless very hard pressed. There was a story current in Hastings at the commencement of the nineteenth century of one Captain Dore – at least, Dore was an assumed name. He was a fine man, full of what Englishmen admire, pluck and daring, and he declared he never would be taken. He was married, and his wife's name was Johanna. He had a remarkably fast sailing cutter called the *Jane*, built by Ransom and Ridley, a ship-building firm once existing in Hastings. It was said of him when he was being pursued, that he would frequently exclaim,"Go along, *Jane*, or Johanna will be a widow." It came to pass that Johanna became a widow, though it was never positively known what became of the captain, his vessel, and crew; it was, however, generally believed that being hard pressed, he scuttled and sank her and all on board, somewhere off the south coast of Ireland.'

The same writer records a fascinating encounter between a revenue cutter and a smuggling boat that could have ended in the death of an innocent bystander:

'An occurrence took place at Hastings about 1816 or 1817. About six pm on a fine summer evening, a gun was heard at sea, and from it a loud report, it seemed not far away. Young and old were soon on the beach, and I, one of the former, with others, saw a sight not quickly to be forgotten.

'It appeared that a lugger had put off from Bexhill; standing out to sea she had been hailed by a frigate, the *Osprey*, and ordered to heave to: this the crew of the lugger refused to do, when a blank cartridge was fired: this not having the desired effect, a shot was fired, and the lugger put about, and made all haste to the shore. The ball fired struck the beach just below the full tide mark, and bounded over the houses about York Buildings, and fell

into a field at the back of the present Wellington Square, very nearly hitting a milkman of the name of Standen. The frigate quickly put out her boats, and followed the lugger ashore, the crew of which made off as quickly as possible. I am not aware what became of them, though I believe one of the party was a man, a native of Bexhill, who was wanted; in fact, who was outlawed for conveying intelligence to the French government of the state of our navy. The captain of the frigate was reprimanded for his conduct.'

A Harsh Code Of Conduct

Banks often mentions the fact that the men recruited to the revenue service were no better than the smugglers themselves. And if the men were bad, their officers were worse – the revenue service was run much as the Navy was run at the time, with the harshest penalties inflicted for the most trivial offences. There is no doubt that the smugglers often defeated the revenue men precisely because government service was always harsh and morale therefore low. The smugglers, by contrast, were free men bound together by family loyalties who made their own rules. Banks and others refer frequently to this difference and to the curious results it sometimes produced:

'In or about 1817, the coast-blockade was instituted, and the officers and men composing that service were stationed round the coast. It is not too much to say that the officers were but little better than the men, and often they were worse. Educated in the school of war, it is perhaps not to be wondered at that they exercised a sort of slave-driving over their men, and a sort of cold bloodedness over any poor devil of a smuggler who came under their clutches.'

Contrast this with his memory of an incident in 1818 when a boat with six men from the revenue cutter, *Camilla* stationed off Hastings, was, in Banks' words 'lost in a dreadful sea, and four perished; but for the generous and humane conduct of a smuggler, who witnessed the catastrophe and took his boat in to help, the others would also have perished.' Here was a case of a smuggler giving the law of the sea – the law which says that rescue comes before everything else – priority over expediency. Other instances of such selfless acts exist both on the side of the smugglers and the excisemen.

A Daring Bit Of Pilotage

Far from Banks' south coast territory, up on the Solway Firth, stories of battles on the high seas are equally common; but few can match the brilliance of the following tale which was handed down through several generations of locals, and was also recorded by John Maxwell Wood in his book *Smuggling on the Solway*, published in 1908. The story tells of a large lugger with a rich cargo that was being out-sailed by a government cutter, and which, by a wonderfully daring and clever bit of pilotage, managed to wrest herself out of her enemy's grasp and to sail off unscathed:

An Essex creek with the mist coming up: perfect smuggling conditions

'Early one morning a richly laden lugger from the Isle of Man was surprised off the Mull of Galloway by the Government cutter under the command of Sir John Reid. The smuggler was running for Cairndoon, on the Glasserton shore of Luce Bay, and disregarding the hail and the order to heave to, set every stitch of canvas, and with a freshening south-western breeze, sped merrily away followed by the cutter also carrying as much sail as she could stagger under. The wind was increasing, but both vessels held on and made no attempt to shorten sail. An eye-witness describes the rate at which they were going as almost incredible. The lugger stood in for the Glasserton shore, closely followed by the cutter, and as the distance between the two vessels was gradually lessening, it was very apparent that unless something turned up in favour of the smuggler he would have to heave to, it being thought impossible that she could round the Burrow Head, whose iron coast and jagged cliffs were at the time, on account of the high wind, causing an extra rapid tide more than ordinarily dangerous.

'But the fearless smugglers' maxim was "Do or die", and after being now carried to the giddy pinnacle of a gigantic wave and anon plunged into a yawning chasm of the mighty deep, the dangerous head was rounded. At length it seemed the weary chase was to end in favour of the Revenue cutter, for when the object of its pursuit was off the Isle of Whithorn, it was observed that she was making for the Isle harbour, as if giving up her attempts to elude her pursuer. The cutter, satisfied that her prey was soon to be in her grasp, shortened sail, and followed into the Isle under easy canvas.

'But what was her surprise on finding, after she had leisurely moored, that no lugger was in the harbour! At the time this incident took place the Isle harbour could be entered by one route and vessels of small tonnage could clear by another. No one would have thought the smugglers' large craft would have attempted to depart by this narrow channel of egress. But owing to the high tide at the time she made the attempt, she succeeded. The chagrin of Captain Reid was of no moderate nature, when on looking through the port he had the mortification of seeing his imagined prize standing away for the English coast all sail set. When the tide receded a few curious seamen at the Isle examined the hazardous route of the lugger in leaving the harbour, and found a track made by the keel of the vessel in the shingly bottom about 100 yards long. Carrying so much sail and having great way on, she had completely forced her passage through the unlikely channel.'

THE RENOWNED CAPTAIN DREW

Occasionally the captain of a revenue cutter is mentioned in admiring terms in an old newspaper article or other document. Stories like this are far rarer, for obvious reasons, than stories of local smuggling heroes, but one such was Captain Drew who hunted smugglers in the far west of Cornwall in the mid-nineteenth century. Captain Drew was master of the *Harpy*.

On 27 September 1840, the *Harpy*, while patrolling in the Channel, captured the *Five Brothers*, a smuggling craft belonging to Cawsand, together with seventy-two half-ankers of foreign spirits which had been thrown overboard by the latter in the course of an exciting chase. The remainder of the cargo was sunk with large stones so that the people of the Harpy could not recover them – though it is more than probable that the inhabitants of Cawsand could, and did, since the fishing up of sunken tubs by means of crooks or creepers was an art which was well known to the smugglers of this date.

In the following week the *Harpy* was successful in capturing, about fifteen miles off the Lizard, another Cawsand vessel called the *Fox*, which had on board 126 half-ankers of contraband spirit, and also four men, including the notorious smuggler Peter Benallack, a tailor of Veryan.

'This,' states the correspondent of the West Briton newspaper 'makes eleven smuggling boats that Lieutenant Drew has taken since he has held command of the *Harpy*, whilst eleven more have been compelled to throw overboard their cargo in order to effect escape when being chased.'

A Heart-Rending Penalty

The penalty now imposed on the smuggler who was caught in the act was certainly severe enough to damp the ardour of all but the most reckless, consisting, as it did, in having his vessel sawn up into three parts. As Commander H. N. Shore remarked in his 1892 book, *Smuggling Days and Ways*, 'the consequent feelings – and language – of the owner, as he watched the slow disintegration of the smart little craft which was the centre of all his hopes, and the source of so much profit, can only be left to the imagination of the reader.'

Respectable Trade

Richard Chaplin of Sudbourn, Suffolk, near Orford, begs leave to acquaint his friends and the public in general, that he has, some time back, declined the branch of smuggling, and returns thanks for all their past favours. – Also, To be SOLD on Monday, August 8th, 1785, at the dwelling house of Samuel Bathers, Sudbourn, the property of Richard Chaplin aforesaid, A very useful CART, fit for a maltster, ashman, or a smuggler – it will carry 80 half ankers or tubs; one small ditto that will carry 40 tubs; also two very good wooden Saddles, three Pads, Straps, Bridles, Girth, Horse-cloth, Corn-bin, a very good Vault, and many articles that are very useful to a Smuggler.

The Ipswich Journal, October 1792

Smuggling Protest

But the main reason for the wide incidence of this free trade was a deeper one: it was to a large extent a protest by the rising middle class – the tradesmen – who resented the continued domination of, and the restrictions imposed by, the old squirearchy or landed gentry. It is significant, too, that this class formed the spear-head in the fight for legitimate free trade later in the nineteenth century.

Quoted from an old newspaper by George Ewart Evans in *Ask the Fellows Who Cut the Hay*

Never a Crime?

'It is impossible,' declared Lord Holland in a speech before the House of Lords, 9 July, 1805, 'totally to prevent smuggling; all that the legislature can do is to compromise with a crime which, whatever laws may be made to constitute it a high offence, the mind of man can never conceive as at all equalling in turpitude those acts which are breaches of clear moral virtues.' Adam Smith in his famous definition of a smuggler as 'a person who, though no doubt highly blamable for violating the laws of his country, is frequently incapable of violating those of natural justice and who would have been in every respect an excellent citizen had not the laws of his country made that a crime which Nature never meant to be so,' states the defence for smuggling with an even greater directness.

Athol Forbes *The Romance of Smuggling*, 1909

Protection Racket

'Batsmen' was a common term among smugglers. The term arose from the fact of their carrying stout ashen poles, five or six ft long, called bats, in the use of which they were as proficient as Robin Hood's men with the quarter staff. They would arrange themselves in rows leading from the beach to the spot where the goods were being stowed, or put into vehicles, and as there were often two or three hundred of them, they defied the blockade men. Afterwards, however, when the blockade men became more determined, they used firearms. But these bats were formidable weapons, and many a fatal blow has been struck by them. It is on record that a man who lived at Icklesham, near Rye, got a blow across the chest from a 'bat' in mistake from a comrade, and died a few hours afterwards.

John Banks *Reminiscences of Old Folkestone Smugglers*, 1885

A Tale of Injustice

Tyrants, wicked monsters, conspirators, inquisitors, nay Devils themselves have had their several apologists; and is a poor smuggler a greater monster than all these? It cannot be denied but the present laws against smugglers are severe and open a wide door for perjuries, false and malicious informations, and great variety of oppression.

The case was this: A man in good circumstances, of a fair character and a large family having the misfortune to be of the same name with an obscure outlaw'd smuggler of the same place, who had absconded, was taken up for him and prosecuted accordingly. His effects were sieged, he remained some months in prison. All the favour he could obtain was Transported for Life. What was the sad consequence? Why truly the husband lost his senses, the wife miscarried and died and the children were all sent to the parish. Certain it is that high duties will eternally tempt men...'

A Free Apology in Behalf of Smugglers, 1749

Cat and Mouse – and Dog

Move and counter move characterise the greatest smuggling period – 1700 to 1850/60 – with the English Preventive Service, as customs was once known, constantly trying to find new ways to catch the increasingly fierce bands of smugglers. There was always a sneaking regard for smugglers of the past. They were the underdogs. The idea that smuggling's romance and glamour is false is itself false. Sailing the channel at night regularly in the days of sail with a cargo of tea or tobacco took great courage and skill – one reason why the preventive men were instructed to capture the smugglers and press them into the Navy. Some smugglers' boats were so well armed that government boats refused to try to stop them!

In Flanders a great deal of smuggling of

French police are suspicious of a female traveller who they suspect is concealing contraband under her skirts

Brabant lace took place. A large dog was used for the purpose; having been shorn of his hair, he was wrapped in priceless lace and then covered with the skin of another dog the same size and colour. His master had only to say 'March, friend' and the beast would run through the gates of Malines or Valenciennes, escape the notice of the officers stationed to intercept smugglers, and would wait outside the gates until followed by his master.

Within five or six years the man had made a fortune, but his neighbours became jealous and suggested smuggling. Even the dog began to realise he was being watched and contrived to elude vigilance. Sometimes he leapt the ramparts and swam the moat, or finding one gate locked or too closely guarded, would try another. But one day he was shot as he swam the moat of Malines; on his body was found lace valued at 5,000 dollars.

William Boys Behrens
Smugglers and Naval Heroes, 1929

Woolly Thinking

In the thirteenth century a tax was levied on wool to prevent its export – the government wanted to keep it in Britain to supply British manufacture. But the high prices paid abroad were greatly tempting, and wool was exported illegally from virtually every town in Sussex and Kent. By Elizabeth I, attempts were made to attract foreign weavers here to prevent the wool leaving. Most of this wool left Romney Marsh, however, and until Charles II, little could be done to prevent this. 1674 was the probable date of the Custom House establishment using sailing craft.

In 1742 George Bridges, who describes himself as 'formerly a wool smuggler', suggested a sort of bill of goods to be signed by the wool carrier. He also knew that it was not just the poor involved: 'Several persons disaffected to the government who, for private ends, meet together and do carry to the seaside great quantities of the wool of these realms for illicit exportation, where it is received, and housed in rooms and cellars belonging to gentlemen of great estates... justices of the peace, rich farmers...

Bridges suggested harsh confiscation – all property from those found in any way connected with the trade.

A Whip for the Smugglers, 1749

Stuffed with Lace

In the early 1800s there were strange doings by night in the creeks and caves and hollow ways of the southern coast, and a remarkable order of passengers by day in the packets from France. Every now and then a fisherman's great boots were found to be stuffed with French lace, gloves and jewellery, or a lady's petticoats to be quilted all through with silk stockings and lace. Here and there a nice-looking loaf of bread was found to have a curious kernel of lace and gloves; and a roll of sailcloth turned out to be a package of gay lute string.

While this was going forward on the English coast, the smugglers on the opposite shore were engaged with much more labour, risk, and expense, in introducing woollens, by a vast system of fraud and lying into the towns, past a series of custom houses. The loss to the revenue was immense. It has been calculated that the loss of duties consequent on smuggling, added to the cost of the preventive service and the Coast Blockade, was not less in 1822 and 1823 than a million a year.

John Banks *Reminiscences of Smugglers and Smuggling*, 1873

Don't Split On Me

Anyone suspected of being a revenue spy was usually found dead, or simply vanished, never to reappear. An informer would be taken to a remote field or beach and held down before being struck on the back of the head by an axe or cutlass. Hence the phrase 'You split on me'. Anyone found like this was known immediately.

A revenue spy would be staked out on the beach at low tide with a red lantern by his head. He was left there till the lantern went out; by then, of course, the tide had come in and he'd drowned. This was known as being redcapped.

Shopkeepers of Broadstairs would listen for news of the first tea clippers of the year passing on their way to London (in September). They'd wait three days and then sell smuggler tea, saying they'd bought it in London. During the Napoleonic wars the French turned a blind eye to smuggling, as the boats provided an easy way to get their spies into England it is said. In Broadstairs the shipbuilders Whites – who'd been there since before the Armada – made ships for the Revenue men *and* for the smugglers. Revenue boats were built for speed: 90ft long, with a beam of 25ft and carrying 12 guns and a crew of 30.

Mounted customs men were known as Hobliers – the reason; they rode Shetland ponies, their feet almost dragging on the ground, the pony appearing continually to 'stumble'. Richard Joy, known as the Kentish Samson, was a smuggler. He was caught but escaped hanging because the King liked him having seen him break thick ropes, carry horses etc. He was made to go into the Navy.'

John Banks *Reminiscences of Old Folkestone Smugglers*, 1885

Constable Caught

In Essex, large-scale smuggling took place mostly between Clacton and Walton. Gin and tea from Holland. Farm workers – scores of them – helped unload. From Wivenhoe it was small scale – tubs of spirits, boxes of tobacco picked up by the fishermen from ships out at sea. Cargo was landed on the marshes between Wivenhoe and Brightlingsea. One Wivenhoe constable was tried and found guilty of smuggling. Customs often sold liquor cheaply when they'd caught a boat, as this advertisement from a local newspaper of about 1830 shows:

'To be sold by inch of candle, to the best bidder, on Monday, the 20th inst at His Majesty's Warehouse at Wivenhoe, six hundred and forty large casks, containing upwards of Five Thousand, Nine Hundred Gallons of Neat Old Bordeaux and Nantes Brandies which will be put up in large and small lots. NB The Brandy will be put up at 5 shillings per Gallon for the Encouragement of Bidders.'

In Folkestone a most notorious woman in smuggling transactions was one named Fox and it fell to her lot to find storage room for 'uncustomed goods' as they termed them. When quite a lass she gave evidence of her fitness for a smuggler's bride by having a single-handed contest with an officer of the revenue. It arose in this way. She was proceeding up the High St. towards what was then the Folkestone Arms, the coaching house, when a few yards from the inn she was met by a custom's house officer, who seeing she had something conceded beneath her big cloak, demanded to see it. 'It's none of your business and you shan't see it,' was the reply and a tussle between the two at once ensued. Some soldiers were loitering in front of the inn, enjoying the fun, but on being summoned to assist the officer, they quickly turned in. Meantime the girl's brother came up and on seeing him, she at once dropped the kegs which the boy seized and ran off with. To prevent her brother being pursued the girl detained the officious exciseman, administering to him a sound thrashing!'

John Banks *Reminiscences of Old Folkestone Smugglers*, 1885

French customs officers in action off Dunkerque, Le Petit Journal, *1905*

THE FIRST AND LAST INN,
LAND'S END, CORNWALL.

The First and Last Smugglers

The inn at Sennen described as 'the resort of all the idle blackguards in the county' was one of the centres of the trade and in 1805 was the scene of a violence. A very valuable cargo had just beenlanded consisting of one thousand gallons of brnady, one thousand gallons of rum, opne thousand gallons of Geneva, and 500 pounds of tobacco. The excise men had appeared and seized the cargo. Quickly a crowd of several hundred gathered and a battle with the excise men took place. At the subsequent trial one Joseph Pollard, a well-known smuggler and part owner of the cargo, was charged with inciting the crowd. The chief witness for the crown was Anne George, a notorious informer whose husband had at one time been landlord of the famous Sennen Inn. The pair had acted as agents in the smuggling business for these profitable ventures. They had then tried to blackmail him by refusing to pay rent for the inn, but when rather foolishly he retaliated by turning them out they unformed against him, and he was sent down to a long term of imprionsment. Several other people suffered the same fate as a sresult of their evidence. However, Anne George was so malicious that little credence could be given to her statements and in the present case Pollard was acquitted.

A.K. Hamilton Jenkin *Cornwall and Its People*, 1970

Platform Ruse

Among the many ingenious schemes resorted to for landing goods, hauling them up the face of the cliff was a favourite. The members of the fraternity residing near Beachy Head, however, have the credit for the following dodge. They disguised themselves as shepherds and under pretence of obtaining seabird's eggs, dug a platform in the face of the cliff, two of them labouring for a week in excavating and levelling the spot. No notice was taken of them, and when the work was completed three or four of them descended unobserved to the platform where they remained perched till dark, and at high water, when the customs men left the beach, a boat was rowed to the foot of the precipice, immediately beneath the platform, and her cargo was leisurely transferred by means of ropes to the platform, and there left securely stowed. The blockademen had been pacing the top of the cliff the whole time, but at too great a distance to hear what was going on and, when the tide went out, they descended as usual to the beach. The coast was then clear for the smugglers to work the casks up to the top of the cliff, which of course was done at night.

John English *Reminiscences of Old Folkestone Smugglers*, 1885

The Villain As Hero

There is the story of Harry Paulet, a Hampshire smuggler, who once made his escape from a French vessel, taking with him a bag of despatches he saw hanging up in a cabin. He mastered their contents and then handed them over to the English Admiralty. On another occasion, returning to England with a cargo of brandy, he sighted the French fleet, which under Admiral Conflans (during the Napoleonic Wars) had stolen out of Brest unperceived. It was a critical moment in our history; it would have been more so had these ships got away. The British Fleet, under Hawke, had been keeping a close blockade, but the elements had combined to thwart him and a terrific gale blew them out of the offing, causing some of the ships to find refuge in Tor Bay. Conflans was anxious to join forces with his supporters before he offered battle to the terrible Hawke.

Paulet was a smuggler, but also a patriot. Noting the number of Conflans' ships and their possible route, he made all sail for the English squadron and upon Hawke's quarter deck made his report. 'If you are telling me the truth,' said the old sea dog, 'I will make your fortune; if you have lied to me, I will hang you up at my yardarm. You may go back to your vessel.' But Paulet was a fighter: 'I should like to have a hand in this battle, sir, if I might remain; you will not find me ungrateful.' The heart of the Admiral went out to the man at once; Paulet was made of the right stuff. The British Fleet immediately weighed anchor and stood out to meet the enemy, which they found and smashed in Quiberon Bay. In this battle Paulet distinguished himself by coolness and courage, and when the fight was done, Hawke sent him home with his pockets full of guineas and with a letter recording the Admiral's grateful thanks.

Athol Forbes *The Romance of Smuggling*, 1909

Napoleon's Bribe

Why did France try to capture English smuggling ships, when so often they were used to send us spies? When a famous smuggler – Will Johnson – was captured he was brought before Napoleon. Napoleon offered him a huge bribe if he would pilot the army of invasion to the English Coast. 'I am a smuggler, but no traitor,' came the reply. There were those who doubted his patriotism, thinking it required a higher bribe. So Johnson was put in prison and told he would remain there until he consented to the demands of his captors.

Athol Forbes *The Romance of Smuggling*, 1909

Jinking The Gauger

From the Union of Scotland with England to the end of the first quarter of the 19th century the Revenue was annually defrauded on a colossal scale by the clandestine importation of foreign spirits and by the unlawful manufacture of spirits at home. All classes of the community participated in the trade: kirk elders, pompous provosts, lairds, baillies and solemn JPs deemed it no sin to 'jink the gauger' or exciseman.

So universal was the infection that the gaugers themselves were often prone to accept bribes on the price of their silence regarding evasions of duty. An illustration of this is found in the story of Sandy Tameson, the St. Andrew's gauger, who, meeting a man on Tentsmuir with a keg of brandy on his shoulder, was thus hailed by the smuggler: 'Maister Tameson, I'm thinking if ye had a crown in either hand, ye coudna tak haud o'th 'keg.' 'That's so', quoth Sandy, 'an if I had anither in my mouth, I coudna speak about it!'

Weekly Scotsman, April 1908

Artfully Concealed

On a boisterous day in October 1822 a cart creaking beneath heavy logs of timber lumbered along the Great North Road between Perth and Kinross. Three stalwart men walked alongside, talking volubly the while in Gaelic. Resting and refreshing man and beast at the last-named town, the cavalcade started forward once again, arriving at North Queensferry late the same evening. There a bargain was struck with the ferryman, and though stormy weather prevailed, the passage was safely effected and men, horse and cart safely landed. From the pier they took the road up the brae by Dalmeny Woods, and travelling as far as Cramond Brig made that their resting place for the night. By four next morning they had breakfasted and were ready for the road when a thunderous knocking at the door alarmed them. To stay their impatient hammerings the host opened and admitted a posse of excisemen. They claimed the men as prisoners and their house and cart with the contents thereof as their property. The smugglers – for such they were – dashed to the rear of the house and fled. Within the hollow interior of the timber logs, which proved to be most carefully built elongated boxes, seventy gallons of fine Highland whisky were artfully concealed and the whole of this, but for an unguarded remark by one of the Highlanders while crossing the firth, would have been disposed of in Edinburgh before break of day.

W. Thomson *The Smuggling Era in Scotland*, 1910

GANG WARFARE

As the result of the widespread protection that smugglers enjoyed at the hands of local people, and the absence of interference at sea owing to the forces of the navy being otherwise requisitioned during the Napoleonic wars, the latter half of the eighteenth century was very much the Golden Age of smuggling. In 1778 Mr Edward Giddy, of Tredrea, Cornwall wrote to the chief custom officer:

'In the western part of this county, smuggling, since the soldiers have been drawn off, has been carried on almost without control. Irish wherries carrying fourteen, sixteen, or more guns, and well manned, frequently land large quantities of goods in defiance of the officers of the customs and excise, and their crews, armed with swords and pistols, escort the smugglers a considerable distance from the sea. In this way, goods are carried from one part of the country to another almost every night. About a fortnight since, a large wherry landed, according to the best information I can obtain, from fifteen hundred to two thousand ankers of spirits (containing 9½ gallons on an average), about twenty tons of tea, and other kinds of smuggled goods, on a sandy beach in Mounts Bay, between the towns of Penzance and Marazion. This beach lies near a public road which, whilst the goods were discharging, was filled with armed men, in order to stop every traveller in whom they could not confide, till the goods were safely lodged in the country.

'A few days after, two officers got information that a very considerable quantity of goods was concealed in the house and premises of a well known smuggler. They obtained from me a search warrant, but were forcibly hindered from executing it by four men, one armed with a pistol and a large whip, the others with sticks and bludgeons. They were told that if they persisted they would have their brains blown out. As the law now stands, I fear a criminal prosecution would have been useless, for the reason, which it shocks me to mention, that a Cornish jury would certainly acquit the smugglers.'

As smuggling developed it inevitably became more organised, and from being largely a family affair in which small groups rarely, if ever resisted arrest, it became more ruthless and bloodthirsty. Powerful gangs grew up and they were often better armed and more numerous than the local bands of customs officials. One instance of the smugglers' daring comes from the pen of A.K. Hamilton Jenkin, author of a now rare Victorian book, *Cornish Seafarers*:

THE CUSTOM-HOUSE IS RAIDED

'By the 1840s, the glory days of Cornish smuggling were over. Nevertheless, the trade continued on a fairly extensive scale, while the smugglers themselves had lost none of their former daring. On 18 September 1840, we learn that the custom-house at Helford, within the port of Gweek, was attacked by a body of men, consisting, as it is supposed, of upwards of thirty persons, who broke open the heavy doors and strong locks, and robbed the cellars of one hundred and twenty-six kegs of contraband brandy (each keg containing four and a half gallons of spirit) which had been seized some days before at Coverack.

'The burglars commenced their work about 1am and in the course of half an hour had succeeded in removing all the kegs except three, which they left for the benefit of the officers at Helford!

'The man and his wife who lived at the custom-house had heard the sound of the cellar doors being broken open, but had been afraid to give the alarm, which, indeed, they could not well have done in any case, as the house was a remote building nearly three-quarters of a mile from any other dwelling. From the tracks of the wheels which were seen next day, it

Outside the Inn *from a painting by Luke Clennel*

was supposed that at least three wagons had been employed in removing the spirit, a fact which accounted for the rapidity with which the whole business had been effected.' The smugglers, however, were no longer in the position of being able to get away with it every time, and the task of bringing the goods to land now involved even more difficulty and danger than that of their subsequent distribution, once they were ashore. Even so, one or two gangs felt so invulnerable that they were able to taunt the excisemen to their faces, explains Mr Hamilton Jenkin:

'An incident which is remembered by the grandparents of persons still living in the town of Redruth involved a band of smugglers who rode into the streets by night, and stopping under the exciseman's window, called forth in mocking tones: "Would 'ee like to see our kags [kegs], maister?"

'Few were *quite* this foolhardy, but many were prepared to make it plain enough that they knew they had the upper hand. At this period, for example, a certain farm in Gwithian parish was a noted haunt of the smugglers. Passing here on a dark night, the traveller would sometimes find the whole place lit up and numbers of horses and ponies tethered outside. It would seem an odd time for a party, although within the house, meat and drink was going in plenty for all who had a mind to it. Not a word would be said at these strangely convivial parties of the work in hand, and a "sarcher" himself might have mingled with the assembly without being one whit the wiser.

'Only when the feasting was over, and news had come that the coast was clear, did a significant nod from the farmer warn the guests that the time had come for action. Mounting his horse, each man betook himself to a certain spot on the cliffs, where the kegs would be found ready laid. Two of these were slung across the back of each horse and every one rode his way. On one occasion, however, a Redruth man (whose family is still resident in the neighbourhood) was pursued by an exciseman.

'Reaching as far as St Erthbridge, he found that his horse was unequal to the burden of himself and the kegs, and accordingly, leaping to the ground, he lashed the animal into a gallop and then ran down and hid himself beneath one of the arches. Not long afterwards, just as he was beginning to feel the water decidedly cold to his feet, he was relieved to hear the thundering hoofs of his pursuer's horse passing overhead. Freed from all further anxiety, he at once came out from his hiding-place and started for his home on foot, to find, on reaching Redruth, that his horse had safely arrived some hours before, together with the precious burden of kegs.'

The Sizewell Gap Gang

On the east coast the extent to which smuggling had become both widespread and — almost — respectable, can be judged from a note in Hansard where an MP spoke in the House of Commons about the fact that 'all the young, clever fellows in Suffolk are

Frenchman's Creek, Cornwall, the inspiration for one of Daphne du Maurier's best-loved tales

employed by smugglers, and have half-a-crown a day while waiting; and when on horse-back, going about the country to dispose of the goods, they have a guinea a day and are well entertained. The gangs are forty to fifty strong and so well horsed that the dragoons could not catch them.'

The notorious Sizewell Gap Gang was comprised of farmers' sons and small trades-men, and their chief enemy was the local squire. Much of this can be gathered from a story in an old newspaper cutting of the time, in which is given an episode in the history of the Sizewell Gap Gang. The date is 1778, but the account must have been written by a mem-ber of the gang a few years later:

'Between Leiston Street and the beach, a distance of about two miles, is a fen or level of marshes called Leiston Common Fen; and it is connected with a Level called Minsmere Level, the upper part of which has been enclosed and is known as Leiston Common Farm. On this farm, held at that time by Mr Doughty an off-hand farm, was a barn; at one end of the barn a stable; over the stable a loft; in which loft there was a wicket window looking into the upper part of the barn; and another looking out abroad through the loft roof. This homestead, which was surrounded by a haulm wall or fence, is nearly two miles from Sizewell Gap. After I had sold my Geneva, the major part of it belonging to Leiston folk, it was stowed away in what in Suffolk is called the goaf – that is, the grain in straw packed ready for threshing; which operation generally finds employment (or used to do before the invention of threshing machines) to one labourer – and in this case Crocky Fellows hap-pened to be the man. In fact the gin was deposited under his care, and to be removed when it was wanted, Mr Doughty never troubling himself about the matter as long as he had brandy, raisins and tea without looking for them.'

Clumpy Bowles Is Caught Stealing

'Now there was a man in the parish called Clumpy, whose name was Bowles, a breeches maker. But the smugglers could never trust him, as he has been found out playing them some slippery trick a year or two before. Bowles had a club-foot; hence his nickname. Crocky was one day looking out at the barn door and spied Mr Clumpy limping along across the Common with a tub of gin, as he suspected, under his arm; and it at once struck him that he had stolen it. He therefore mounted the goaf and found somebody had been there as the bar-ley was disarranged and a tub had gone. Crocky in an instant decided how to act, for he con-cluded Bowles would soon be there again; and he was not wrong in his conjecture.

'Thumping away at his work and keeping his ears open, in about an hour he heard a rustling overhead; dropping his flail, he sprang up the bracket of the cross-beam and on to the goaf in a moment. There was Clumpy crouched in a corner and the stable window wide open. Crocky, approaching him, exclaimed: "I'll gin you, you scamp!"

'And suiting his action to the word, gave Clumpy what in Suffolk is called a clout of the skull; and catching him by the collar, hurled him clean over the large beam of the barn down to the threshing floor below enough to break his neck, but for the straw and barley on which Crocky had been at work. The other jumped down and would have commenced pummelling him again, but Bowles swore he would go and lay an information against the goods; and Crocky thought better to desist.'

Bowles Turns Informer

'Bowles left the barn threatening and swearing, and Crocky went up and shut the window; and locking up the barn went into the village to call a council to know what was to be done. The owners of the hidden cargo were soon assembled; and some thought Bowles would be afraid to inform; and some thought otherwise. But the conclusion was that the goods should be removed as soon as night came on; when an accidental sight of Bowles by one of the party in close discourse with old Read, the preventive officer, accelerated the moment and all hands set to work.

'At that time there were two horse-soldiers at Leiston White Horse; two at East Bridge public house, about two miles off; and no more nearer than Snape Crown or Aldbro. The Leiston soldiers were both drunk; and Read – or Old Billy, as he was called – was lame; and he told Clumps he must go to East Bridge for the the soldiers there. Off set Bowles limping along as fast as he could; but if any of the smugglers had known his errand, he would never have got to the Elephant and Castle; but he did arrive there; and by the greatest chance in the world found the soldiers. The landlady, seeing something was amiss, called the soldiers into the back room and gave to each two large glasses of Hollands to keep out the cold; for it was a bitter cold day. And this, with the glass they took on their own account before starting, made them about as sober as their comrades at Leiston were.

'By the time old Read had mounted his horse and the soldiers had got ready to go, it was three o'clock in the afternoon; and the smugglers were prepared by the time the Government men arrived. It was dark. Clumps kept out of the way, for he was now frightened at his own folly. Just as the officers and soldiers entered the barn yard, Crocky had put a large padlock on the door.

' "I demand admittance to this barn!" says Mr Read.

' "What for?" says Crocky.

' "To search for smuggled goods," was the reply.

' "I shall let no man pull my master's property about without his leave," says the other. "Then I must order the soldiers to knock the lock off."

' "Knock and be damned," says Fellows, "if you can; but I'll knock down the first man who touches that lock!"

'And one of the soldiers took hold of the lock as if to examine it. Crocky struck him on the breastbone and drove him back. At this instant, Sam Newson of Middleton and a maltster of the name of Wil Thornton, a great cross-made fellow, entered the barn yard; and Thornton, who was called Quids from his immoderate use of tobacco, stood behind Crocky. Sam Newson began to wrestle with another soldier; and thus an hour was spent in fighting, laughing, tumbling about and swearing at one another in fun and pelting each other with barn-door litter. At length a little fellow, a tailor in the village, came and spoke a few words to Crocky, who immediately unlocked the door with the remark that if his master had no objection he had none.'

The King's Men Are Outwitted

'The whole party entered and one of the soldiers scrambled up the goaf (the hay). "Here's the nest,' said he; "but, by God, the eggs are all gone!" "Why do you say so," says Old Billy who made an attempt to get up but could not manage it.

'The soldiers were all busy looking about when Sam Newson having been up the stable loft and fastened the wicket on the other side, now came and spoke to Fellows, who slyly slipped out. Shutting the barn door he made the whole of the King's men prisoners. Locking them all in, he and Newson went and themselves made sure the tubs were all gone: and then returned and released the party.

'Read, who saw the trick had been played by removing the goods while his men were engaged in the barn yard, told the soldiers it was plain there was nothing to seize, and they were dismissed. The fact is that the tubs were handed in silence by about twenty smugglers into six two-horse carts and drove clean away to Cold Fair Green, and there deposited in a cart-shed until midnight, when they were carried right back to the barn and placed in a large vault in the barn yard under a dunghill or, as the Suffolk people call it, a muckheap. About six or eight score of sheep were driven in about the place to obliterate all signs of any other footing than their own. The tubs were piled on each side the vault, and a passage left in the middle at the further end of which was stowed some bales of tobacco and tea; the whole being shut up by a trap door at one end, to get at which a portion of the long horse-muck had to be cut away with a hay knife – this being the mode of concealing goods in the long winter nights against they might be wanted in the summer.

'They were now in a place of safety, and the next thing the smugglers turned their attention to was to prevent any male informing.'

Bowles Is Given His Come-Uppance

'About a fortnight after the circumstances I have related took place, one night about nine o'clock, a couple of very tall, stout men stopped their horses at the door of the cottage where Bowles lived, which was a small house standing in a sand pit close by the Yoxford turnpike, and about a hundred yards from Leiston Street. One of the men alighted, and opened tbe cottage door: he found all the inmates in a state of terror, as they had heard the horses stop.

' "Is Bowles within?" said the man. "No," replied the poor old woman, his landlady. "It's a lie" said the fellow, and he strode across the room and, opening the closet door under

Smugglers defend themselves vigorously against an attack by Revenue Men

the staircase, he forced the screaming, trembling wretch across the room to the door, where the other man sat on horseback. He caught hold of Bowles's arm and jerked him into the pummel of the saddle, his head on one side and his heels on the other. Having got him secure, he struck the spurs into his horse's sides, and the other mounting directly, set off at full gallop through Leiston Street into a lane which leads to Cold Fair Green; and there they dismounted.

'One man thrust the end of his whip into Bowles's mouth, and the other directly forced the bung of a beer cask in between his teeth, and tied it fast round his head with his neckerchief. They then took his head on one horse and the other took his feet. They then flogged the poor wretch with their heavy whips from Leiston through Friston, Snape, Dunningworth and Blax hall. Five or six miles at least did they keep on with their barbarity, till they were tired; and then they threw what they supposed to be his dead body over the hedge into a plantation of Squire Shepherd's at Campsey Ash, where he was found by a labourer's dog next morning to all appearance lifeless. But the husbandman, seeing the state he was in, unbound his head; procured assistance; and had him conveyed to Tunstall Green Man, where an incident occurred which had the effect of bringing the two ruffians to justice.

'The countryman who found Bowles went on the Sunday morning to see how he was, and was admitted to his bedroom, where he had been attended at Squire Shepherd's expense; and who had ordered everything for him his forlorn state required. For the gentlemen of the neighbourhood took the matter up and were determined to bring the actors to justice if possible. In the course of conversation the man pulled the bung out of his pocket to show Bowles what it was. The girl of the house, being in the room at the time, took the bung to look at it, and exclaimed: "Why, dear me! If that is not the bung Tom Tibbenham asked me to lend him last Monday! I'll swear to it, for I cut the notch on it to know which cask it belonged to!"

'The countryman said to the lass: "Just stop with this poor man a minute or two." He had seen Mr Shepherd ride into the yard, and did not want the girl to see anybody till Mr S had seen her. She did as he requested; and the man asked the Squire into the room, where an examination of Bowles took place; he declared the men to be Debney and Tibbenham; as he knew them both, having often seen them at Leiston White Horse, and in their smuggling vocations.'

The Smugglers Are Apprehended

'The consequence of this information was a warrant issued against each of them; and both were apprehended the same day in the neighbourhood. They were fully committed on the girl's evidence, in conjunction with Bowles's assertion, to Woodbridge Bridewell. It appears they thought very lightly of the matter, as Cleaver – that is, Tibbenham – who was a butcher, admitted the fact in a boasting sort of way and declared if it had not been for Nosey (Debney) he would have served the bloody informer ten times worse.

The smugglers alarmed – but if the goods were well hidden they would be sure to brazen it out

'After they were put in confinement, it was found necessary to send Bowles right away; and he went to London till the trial, when the poor girl, who had got into a sad mess, gave her evidence and Bowles gave his. And the two fellows were sentenced to two years' imprisonment in Ipswich gaol. Bowles quitted the country, and I don't think he ever returned to it, as I have never been able to learn anything of him since.'

Cooper And Debney Are Smothered

'To return to the goods which were deposited in the vault: they happened to be wanted in a short time after the circumstance occurred. A party of smugglers, among whom was a brother of Debney called Sam, and a young fellow of the name of Will Cooper from Tunstall, assembled to work the goods as it was termed; and had three or four carts with horses fit to remove them. Crocky Fellows was among them and directed whereabouts to cut the muckheap to find the door, which was soon uncovered and opened; and the owners were there of course to deliver them, the same as if it had been a warehouse. As soon as the door was opened Crocky said: "You had better let the foul air get out!"

'But Cooper, with an oath, replied: "I have enough good stuff in me to repel all the foul air in the world!" And he and Debney scrambled down the steps which were nearly perpendicular under the trap door and about sixteen feet deep. The moment they were down all was silent; and Stokes, who was there, called to them but received no answer. A man called Nichols, or Black George, now attempted to go down; but he had just got his head level with the roof of the vault when he held up his arm: Stokes caught it and lugged him out; and he fell down on the ground insensible. The whole party now fell to work, and the heap was soon removed, and the roof torn off but it was too late! Cooper was found lying flat on his face at the farther end of the vault, and Debney standing leaning on the gin tubs, about halfway along the passage – both dead and their faces blood-shot and red as fire.

'As soon as they had laid the bodies into one of the carts, they took the gin, tobacco and tea and conveyed them away, paying but little regard for the concealment, as they were all horror struck about the dreadful disaster which had befallen them.

'The bodies were taken to Tunstall, and I never knew whether a coroner's inquest went over them, or how it was ordered; but they both lie in one grave; and a large gravestone, nearly in front of Tunstall Church Park and near the road was erected to perpetuate their memory, and so far as I know still remains. I was not at the time in Suffolk, but I had the following particulars from a friend who was pretty well amongst them all the time.

'He tells me that it was about twenty of the most desperate of the smugglers swore to punish Bowles; and Debney and Tibbenham took the job in hand of their own accord, and at their own opportunity. And the whole seemed to be unfortunate, for the same evening that Cooper and Debney were smothered, old Ingall, an exciseman living at Saxmundham, having heard of the death of the two men, concluded that there would be a removal of the liquor, as it was no secret there was some; and he thought he could make a seizure.

'The smugglers had for some years paid a man of the name of Isaac Mayhew, who lived opposite to Ingalls, to watch him of an evening; and when he saw him go to his stable and take his pistols from a hole bored in the gable end of the house, saddle his horse himself, which he could do, Isaac knew that he was going out after the smugglers. A man was always posted at a preconcerted spot, to whom Isaac repaired with the intelligence; the man in turn told the smugglers; and Ingall almost always returned disappointed.'

Exciseman Isaac Seizes The Goods

'On the night in question, Isaac could not find the man, and none came. And the exciseman took the two Saxmundham soldiers with him; and, knowing all the haunts of the smugglers, as it happened, went right to the spot at Aldringham Parrot. In the yard he made a seizure of six carts, twelve horses, and 300 tubs of gin without the least resistance. The smugglers for the time appearing terror-struck, he got to the excise office at Saxmundham with them; and a short time after, the tubs – as it was the custom at that time – were staved in the yard and the liquor all thrown away. And on this occasion which was the last that it was poured down, it ran out of the Custom-house yard; and the people dug a hole outside the gate and carried away the gin in pails – dirt and all. And one man drank so much of the filthy mixture before it had time to settle that he died the same night. Isaac Mayhew lost his berth as watcher, because he was suspected of being paid by both parties and informing when he had an opportunity. I think that I could call this lot of goods by no more appropriate name than The Doomed Cargo.'

The father of the Debney brothers farmed in Tunstall where the two smugglers lie buried; Cooper's family were millers. The tomb inscription of the two dead men reads:

In Memory of ROBERT DEBNEY and WILLIAM COOPER
who departed this life the 22nd of June, 1778. RD aged 28 & WC 18 years.
All you, dear Friends, that look upon this Stone,
Oh think how quickly both these Lives were gone.
Neither Age nor Sickness brought them to the clay;
Death quickly took their Strength and Sense away.
Both in the Prime of Life they lost their Breath,
And on a Sudden were cast down by Death.
A cruel Death that could no longer spare
A loving Husband nor a Child most dear.
The loss is great to those they left behind,
But they thro' Christ, 'tis hop'd, true Joys will find.

The inscription gives Debney's age as twenty-eight; but after the parish registers had been examined it was found that he was, in fact, thirty when he died.

'In Danger Of Their Lives'

If there was a dark side to the smuggling trade when it reached gang level, it must also be remembered that if the smugglers were armed men, so in like manner were those whose business it was to prevent smuggling. And if, under such circumstances, the conflicts which were bound to take place resulted in bloodshed, and occasionally even loss of life, neither side could be held solely responsible. In most cases, however, it was the smugglers' reputation which suffered. For example in the year 1735, a quantity of rum which had been discovered in a barn near Fowey was being taken to the custom house, and we read that the excisemen were attacked by an armed body of smugglers: the latter had acquired such a reputation for violence in that district that, in the words of the official report 'If the officers attempt to make any seizure they go in danger of their lives, the smugglers having entered into a combination to rescue any person who shall be arrested.'

How far the words 'go in danger of their lives' should bear a literal interpretation it is difficult to say, seeing that the report, being an official one, must necessarily have been somewhat biased. Nevertheless, there is plenty of evidence to show that serious clashes between the government officers and large numbers of the local population – most of whom were involved with the smugglers anyway – were at one time frequent.

The Violence Increases

During the time of the coast-blockade, when the smugglers were at last beginning to lose the upper hand, affrays between the runners and the blockademen were frequent and bloody. Nearly the last of those blood-sheddings took place on 3 January 1828, near Bexhill in Sussex. According to the account of one of those who took part – an account recorded by John Banks in his *Reminiscences of Old Folkestone Smugglers* – it all began when a cargo of goods was landed at Mr Brooks' farm. It was a moonlit night, the moon being in the last quarter. The tubs of spirits were loaded on men's shoulders and in carts. A noted smuggler, and a native of Bexhill, was captain of the boat.

The coast-blockade from Galley Hill Tower tried to intercept the smugglers, but finding themselves too weak for the purpose (the smugglers being armed, and having likewise with them sixteen or eighteen batsmen – men armed with clubs), they obtained reinforcements that raised their number to about forty men. They came up with the smugglers near Sidley, and here the armed smugglers and the batsmen drew themselves up in regular line, and a desperate fight took place.

In the first onset a quarter-master named Collins was killed. Two batsmen were also killed; the body of one named Smithurst was carried and laid in the barn of Cramp's Farm. When his body was found, his bat was still grasped in his hands, and it had almost been hacked in pieces by the cutlasses of the blockademen. The goods were all got away, as were all the wounded. One of the wounded men, named P , was taken to his home, a lonely house near Windmill Hill; the surgeon who attended him would take his horse to a gentleman's

The Downs at East Dean, Eastbourne

stables in the neighbourhood, put it up there, and then quietly walk across the fields to the house where his patient was lying. The smuggler became a cripple for life.

Between seven and eight o'clock in the morning in October 1830, a boat came in close to the library at St Leonards. The company, that had evidently been in waiting all the night, rushed to the beach, and told the preventive-man on duty that they would not hurt him if he remained quiet. He fired his pistol, at which they began to beat him, and would have severely injured him but for the interference of some gentlemen who were on the spot. One hundred and fifty casks of spirits were got away. The boat was abandoned.

On 3 January 1831, on a fine moonlit night, either through some misunderstanding on the part of the smugglers, or through some information having been given, a serious affray took place near the Dripping Well at Fairlight. Three of the company were shot, a young man, George Harrod (who was also run through with a bayonet), and William Cruttenden (Trucks); the latter was found the next morning in the New Barn Field, close by – it was then a turnip field, and for a considerable distance round where the body was found, the tops were knocked to pieces, showing that the poor fellow must have died a terrible death. The young man was seriously wounded in the thigh. He was taken to a house near the Fish Ponds, and two medical gentlemen, Robert Ranking and Ross Chapman, were sent for from Hastings to attend to him. When they arrived at the house they found it strictly guarded by a party of marines, who at that time were assisting the coast-blockade. The officer in charge of course wanted to know their errand, and demurred at their being allowed to enter the house. Mr Ranking, however, maintained that they were sent for to attend a woman in labour, that it was a very serious case, and that he should hold the officer responsible if anything went wrong; so the guard was withdrawn, and they were both allowed to go on their errand of mercy. The young man partially recovered, and was afterwards smuggled into Hastings.

During this encounter the blockademen apparently fired at anything they saw moving, while the marines fired into the air, their officer charging them not to hurt the smugglers.

John Banks, who was an authority on the history of Hastings, goes on to list a number of other serious affrays involving large numbers of men:

'On the 22nd of February, 1832, between two hundred and three hundred men assembled at Worthing, William Cowardson, a Coast guardsman, was shot, and several more carried away wounded.

'On the 23rd of January, 1833, the Eastbourne smugglers having killed the chief-boatman, George Pett, formed two lines on each side, till the cargo was run – several of their party were wounded, but none of them discovered.

'Thomas Monk, a poor fiddler of Winchelsea, was shot on the Ist April, 1838, by the Coast-guard, in an affray at Camber Castle. This was the last occasion on which a life was sacrificed.'

The foregoing extracts, some of which were obtained from eye-witnesses, show in a striking manner the immense extent of smuggling transactions.

THE PREVENTIVE SERVICES

It seems incredible, now, how such a state of things could have grown up; however, high protective duties were the chief cause, and certainly once it was found that smuggling didn't pay, it ceased to flourish. The lowering of import duties in fact did more to prevent smuggling than all the custom-house officers, coast-blockade, and coastguard put together. Another matter which may seem to deserve explanation is, why did so many serious affrays take place between the coastguard and the smugglers during the latter years of smuggling? The answer I suspect has to do with the fact that during the wars with France, the custom-house officers ashore, and the preventive service afloat were too busy to notice a smuggling transaction till they broke their shins against the tubs; then a percentage was agreed upon and the rest let go, so that not uncommonly they were as deep in the mud as the smugglers were in the mire. At the end of the wars when the coast-blockade were put on, things were altered. The coast-blockade consisted of men drafted from ships of war, no longer wanted as sailors, the war being over; they went about their work in a rough bull-dog sort of fashion.

Fishermen in a Cove at Sunset *by Pietro Barucci*

They went out heavily armed, and were not slow in using their arms; for instance if they wanted to enter a house in which they suspected any smuggler was concealed, they would unceremoniously smash open the door with the butt-ends of their muskets, and when inside would bundle women and children, bed and all, onto the floor.

This incensed the smugglers, who imagined that, having bought goods and paid for them, in running them they were only securing their own property. They then took to arming themselves, first with clubs seven or eight feet long, and then with fire-arms. When the coastguard superseded the coast-blockade, things improved; and the lowering of import duties finally put an end to smuggling altogether.

The coast-blockade always carried a brace of pistols, and in the night a cutlass and a musket and bayonet. The coast-blockademen were open (some of them) to bribes.

THE HAWKHURST GANG

Perhaps the most serious – and probably the most famous – smuggling affray occurred many years earlier, in the mid-eighteenth century. From a work first published in 1749 we learn of the notorious Hawkhurst Gang, without some account of which, no book on smuggling would be complete. However, although it is excellent, blood-curdling stuff, this much-retold story is curious for a number of reasons. First there is the slightly suspicious emphasis on senseless cruelty: the smugglers don't just kill their victims, they slowly whip them to

Pistols used by the Hawkhurst gang

death or almost to death; like many penny-dreadful pamphlets of the time, the accounts give one the impression that all this is designed to make a good read rather than to convey accurately what went on.

Nothing is said about the goods the gang smuggled; nor how they had managed to carry on their trade so long if they were locally hated and feared: all the emphasis is on the fact that they are simply bloodthirsty criminals. Towards the end we are told by the anonymous author that they hit an old woman merely because she was old. By contrast, when the local gentry are mentioned the writer's tone is embarrassingly ingratiating. One almost senses the hand of the authorities in all this: it is, in other words, a piece of propaganda – but fascinating for all that. Here is the story:

'In September 1747, one John Diamond, otherwise Dymar, agreed with a number of smugglers to go over to Guernsey to smuggle tea; having purchased a quantity and returning in a cutter, they were chased, and the vessel and tea taken by one Captain Johnson, the crew escaping in a boat; Captain Johnson carried the vessel and tea to the port of Pool, and lodged the tea in the custom-house there.

'The smugglers were very much annoyed at the miscarriage of their purchase, and they resolved not to sit down contented with their loss; a consultation was held, and it was agreed that they would go and remove the tea from the warehouse in which it was lodged.'

The King's Custom-House Is Raided

'Accordingly, in about the middle of the following month, a body of them, to the number of sixty, well armed, assembled in Charlton Forest, in the County of Sussex and started on their enterprise: about thirty of the gang were stationed at different places as scouts, to watch the movements of the officers and soldiers, and to be ready to assist or alarm the main body, in case any opposition should be made to their daring scheme.

'In the night-time between the 6 and 7 October, they went to Pool, about thirty of them being present, broke open the custom-house (notwithstanding that an armed sloop-of-war lay off the town) and took away all the tea, except one bag of about 5lb.

'Passing through Fordingbridge in Hampshire, the next morning they were seen by some hundreds of people, who assembled to view the cavalcade. Among the spectators was one Daniel Chater, a shoemaker, who was known to Diamond, one of the gang, they having formerly worked together in harvest time. Diamond shook hands with Chater as he passed along, and threw him a bag of tea.'

The Authorities Take Action

'Such a daring piece of business as breaking open the King's custom-house could not, of course, go unnoticed by the authorities, so accordingly His Majesty issued his proclamation offering a reward for the apprehending of any of the persons concerned in the offence. Diamond was taken into custody on suspicion, and Chater was apprehended because he had mentioned in conversation with his neighbours that he knew Diamond, and that he had seen him go by with the gang the day after the custom-house was broken open – and because this had come to the knowledge of the collector of customs at Southampton, the latter was ordered to send William Galley, a custom-house officer, with Chater, with a letter to Major Battin, a Justice of the Peace for the County of Sussex, in order that Chater might be examined as to what he knew of the matter, and to ascertain if he could prove the identity of Diamond's person.

'Accordingly on Sunday 14 February 1748, they set out on horseback for Chichester; passing through Havant, they called on an acquaintance of Chater's and told him where they were going, and he informed them that Major Battin was at East Marden near Chichester and directed them to go by Stanstead, near Rowland's Castle. Pursuing their journey, they called at the New Inn, at Leigh, and asked the nearest way; they saw

George and Thomas Austin, two brothers, and their brother-in-law Mr Jenkes, and as they were going the same way, these three said they would show them, and they accordingly set out together, all being on horseback.'

The Smugglers Are Warned

'About twelve at noon, they arrived at the White Hart, at Rowland's Castle, a house kept by one Elizabeth Payne, a widow who had two sons, both smugglers, but who followed the occupation of blacksmiths in the same village. Mrs Payne, suspecting that the journey of Galley and Chater boded no good to the smugglers, sent one of her sons for William Jackson and William Carter, two smugglers who lived near her house. While her son was gone, Galley and Chater wished to be going, and asked for their horses; Mrs Payne, to detain them, said the man who had the key of the stable was out. Jackson and Carter soon came in, and Mrs Payne communicated to them her suspicions concerning Galley and Chater; soon after she advised George Austin to go away about his business, as she respected him, and by staying he might come to some harm; he left, but his brother and brother-in-law remained.

'During this time Mrs Payne's other son came in, and finding that there were grounds to suspect that the two strangers were going to inform against the smugglers, he went out and fetched William Steele, Samuel Downer – otherwise Samuel Howard, otherwise Little Sam – Edmund Richards, Henry Sheerman – otherwise Little Harry – all smugglers, and all belonging to the same gang.

'After they had drunk a little while, Jackson took Chater aside into the yard, and asked him how he was, and where Diamond was. Chater said he believed he was in custody; that he was going to appear against him, for which he was sorry, but that he could not help it. Galley thinking that Jackson was persuading Chater not to give information against the smugglers, desired him to come in, when Jackson with an oath, gave him a blow in the face, and knocked him down. Galley said he was a king's officer and would not put up with such usage; Jackson again offered to strike him, but was hindered by one of the Paynes, who said, "Don't be such a fool, do you know what you are doing?"

'Galley and Chater began to be very uneasy, and wanted to be going, but Jackson, Carter and the rest persuaded them to stay and have more drink, and make it up, saying they were sorry for what had happened.

'Unfortunately for Galley and Chater, they were persuaded, and stayed drinking with all present. Jackson and Carter after a while wanted to see the letter they were taking to Major Battin, but they refused to show it; whereupon the former made a resolution that they would see it, and for that purpose plied them well with drink till they and Thomas Austin were completely fuddled; then they persuaded Galley and Chater to go into another room in which was a bed, and lie down: they did so, and from the effects of the liquor, were soon fast asleep; the letter was then taken out of one of their pockets, brought into the kitchen, and read by one of the party – and the contents of it being plainly a design to promote an information against some of the gang, they agreed first to destroy the letter, and then consulted what to do with the men.'

The Smugglers Cruelly Torture Their Victims

'And now began a series of cold-blooded, cruel and barbarous acts, the bare recital of which makes one's blood curdle, and which, were the facts not well authenticated, would lead persons to doubt if human beings in a civilised country could be found to put in practice such a piece of diabolical savageness.

'Galley and Chater being still asleep on the bed, one of the smugglers, Jackson, putting on his spurs, got on the bed, and spurred them on their foreheads to wake them, and then whipped them with his horsewhip so that they both came into the kichen bloody. They then placed the two men on horseback, both on the same horse, each man's legs being tied beneath the horse's belly, and then their four legs tied together; and one of the smugglers, Richards, threatened to shoot anyone who should mention anything that was being done.

'They then set out, all on horseback, except two – John Race, who had joined the party; he stayed behind, not having a horse – and William Steele, who led the horse on which Galley and Chater were; the roads being bad, their progress was very slow. They had not gone above one hundred yards before Jackson, who seems to have been a ringleader in the diabolical business, called out: "Whip 'em; cut 'em, slash 'em, damn 'em," and then all except Steele set to lashing and cutting them over the head, face, eyes, shoulders, or wherever they could injure them most, till, unable to bear the anguish of this terrible punishment, the poor men rolled from side to side, till at last they fell with their heads under the horse's belly, in which posture their heads were frequently struck with the horse's feet. This happened at Wood's Ashes, about half a mile from the place where the whipping began. They were placed upright, and the same treatment continued to Goodthrop Dean, about half a mile farther, when they fell as before, their heads under the horse, and their heels up in the air.'

The Murder Of Galley

'The men were now become so weak that they could no longer sit upon the horse – they were therefore separated, and Galley put up behind Steele, and Chater behind little Sam. In passing through the village of Dean, Jackson swore he would shoot either of them who made any noise. They then went to a well near Lady-Holt Park, where they swore they would murder Galley, by throwing him down the well. Galley more dead than alive from the treatment he had received, begged them to despatch him at once, when Jackson, with a fearful oath, said, "No, if that's the case, we must have something more to say to you." They again put him on a horse, and fell to whipping him all the way over the downs, till, being no longer able to sit on the horse, they laid him across the saddle, and Richards got up behind to hold him on, and thus they carried him above a mile farther, when Richards, tired of holding him on, let him fall by the side of the horse.

'Again putting him on a horse, not sitting, but lying, and being held first by one, and then by another of the smugglers, they proceeded a mile or two farther, when Little Harry, who had mounted behind Galley to hold him, the poor fellow, finding he was falling, cried out, "I fall, I fall, I fall!" Little Harry, giving him a push as he was falling said, "Fall, and be damned": upon which he fell, and they thought he had broken his neck, and was dead.

'During the whipping which had taken place, to make it more effectually felt, the smugglers had taken off Galley's great-coat, which was found in the road next morning, all bloody.

'Supposing now that Galley was dead, they laid him across a horse, one on each side holding him on, and another leading the horse. They brought him to the house of one Pescod, a reputed smuggler who, however, suspecting some evil work and being ill in bed, refused to admit them. It being now between one and two o'clock in the morning, they agreed to go to one Scardefield's, at the Red Lion, at Rake, who, after many refusals, at length admitted them, made them a fire in the parlour, and supplied them with liquor.

'Scardefield, seeing Galley in the brewhouse lying apparently dead, and Chater in the parlour, standing up, very bloody, was informed, upon enquiring the cause, that they had had an engagement with some officers, and had lost their tea, and were afraid that some of their people were killed. This was said to conceal the murder of Galley, and to account for the bloody appearance of Chater.

'After drinking pretty freely, they all went out, taking Galley, or his corpse, if he was quite dead, which is doubtful, with them. Two of them, Carter and Richards, returned to ask Scardefield if he could find the place where they had before hidden some goods. He said he could, but refused to go with them. They insisted that he should, and Carter, taking a candle and lanthorn, and a spade, they went to where the others of the party were waiting; when they dug a hole, and in this hole they buried Galley.

'Having disposed of Galley's body they returned to Scardefield's, where they sat carousing the best part of Monday, and during the time they were there, one Richard Mills came in. This Richard Mills was the son of old Richard Mills, to whose house they had conveyed Chater, and chained him by the leg in an out-house called a skilling, a place in which they laid up turf, old Mills being at the time a turf-cutter; in this place Chater was looked after by Little Harry and old Mills.

'After drinking all that day, Monday, at Scardefield's, they separated, so that by being at their respective homes on Tuesday, their neighbours might have no suspicion of the business they had in hand; they agreed to meet at the same place on Wednesday evening, which they accordingly did. At this meeting were present William Jackson, William Carter, William Steele (afterwards king's evidence), Edmund Richards, and Samuel Howard, alias Little Sam, five of the six who were concerned in the murder of Galley. Also there were John Cobby, William Hammond, Benjamin Tapner, Thomas Stringer, Daniel Perryer alias Little Daniel, John Mills, Thomas Willis, Richard Mills jun., and John Race (another king's evidence), fourteen in number. (Richard Mills, senior, and Little Harry stayed at home to take care of Chater.) They dropped in, one after another, as if by accident, so that it was late at night before they all got together.'

The murder of Galley and Chater in a nineteenth-century etching by 'Phiz'

The Murder Of Chater

'Being all assembled, they consulted what was to be done with Chater; one proposed one thing, another, another; at length it was finally determined to take him to Harris's Well, near the Lady-Holt Park, in which they had previously intended to put Galley, and there put him out of existence.

'While this consultation was going on, Tapner and Cobby went to the turf-house where Chater was chained by the leg, and inflicted on him unheard-of cruelties. Tapner, in particular, pulling out a large clasp knife, expressed himself thus: "Down on your knees, and go to prayers, for with this knife I will be your butcher." Poor Chater expecting then and there to be murdered, fell on his knees, and offered up prayers to God in the best manner his pain and anguish would allow him. During this, when it might be supposed even a fiend would relent for a few minutes at least, Cobby got behind him and kicked him in the small of the back, while Tapner, with the feelings of a demon, hacked him across the forehead, eyes and nose with his clasp-knife.

'The smugglers having agreed how to dispose of Chater, they all, with the exception of the Millses, set out to take him and despatch him at Harris's Well, as being in their way towards their respective homes, and therefore not likely to be any hindrance to them on their journey. Chater was then set on Tapner's horse and taken towards the well, Tapner whipping him over the face and eyes, causing his wounds to bleed copiously, and swearing at the same time, that "if he blooded his saddle he would destroy him that moment, and send his soul to hell."

'At the dead of the night, and being so near the middle of it that it was uncertain whether it was Wednesday night or Thursday morning, they arrived at the well. The well was between twenty and thirty feet deep, and fenced round with a paling fence to prevent cattle falling in. Being come up to the fence, they dismounted Chater; and Tapner, taking a cord from his pocket, made a noose at one end, and fastened it round Chater's neck. They bade him get over the fence to the well. The poor man observing an opening where a pale or two had been broken away, made an attempt to get through; but, being in the opinion of the smugglers so heinous an offender, this favour was too great to be allowed him, and they compelled him, weak as he was, his wounds gaping, and being ready to faint through loss of blood, to get over the pales as well as he could.

'Being over, Tapner fastened the end of the rope that was round his neck to the rail of the fence, for the well had neither lid, kirb nor roller. The rope being fixed, they all got over and pushed him into the well; but the rope being short, his legs only hung into it, and his body leant back towards the fence. Finding that the weight of his body was not sufficient to strangle him, Stringer, with the assistance of Cobby and Hammond, pulled his legs out of the well; then Tapner untied the cord, and they threw him, or rather let him fall into the well, head foremost.

'After this they stood by the well for some time, and it being the dead of the night, and everything still, they heard him breathe or groan, and were thence assured that he was still alive. Fearing that any casual passer-by might hear him, they procured a ladder from one William Combleach, a gardener who lived but a little way off, intending to go down into the well and despatch him. They told Combleach that one of their companions had fallen into the well, and that they wanted the ladder to get him out; he thinking to do a charitable action, lent them the ladder, which they carried to the well; but whether from the confusion in which they were, or from the horror of the dreadful work in which they had been engaged, they could not, though six of them were employed in doing it, raise the ladder high enough to get it over the pales.

'Finding their efforts ineffectual to raise the ladder over the fence, and hearing the poor fellow still groaning, they set about thinking what other means were left to despatch him; and recollecting, they hunted about till they found two heavy logs of wood that had been gate-posts. These they threw into the well, and then resolving to do their business effectually, they got together as many great stones as they could find, and threw them into the well. And now hearing nothing of the unfortunate man, though they listened attentively, they concluded that he was quite dead, mounted their horses, and went to their respective homes.

'Previously, however, they had consulted what was to be done with the two living witnesses against them, namely the two horses that had been ridden by Galley and Chater, and they had agreed, after many plans had been suggested and abandoned, to kill them and take off their skins. Accordingly they killed the one, a grey on which Galley had ridden, flayed him, and cut up his hide into small pieces; but when they came to look for the other, a bay on which Chater had ridden, he was not to be found; he had got away, and was soon after delivered to his rightful owner; but the grey, which had been hired for Galley by Mr Shever of Southampton, was obliged to be paid for by him.'

William Galley, brought cross a Horse to a Sand Pit where a deep Hole is Dug to Bury him in

The unfortunate William Galley put by the Smugglers into the Ground & as is generally believed before he was quite DEAD.

Suspicions Are Aroused

'The long absence of Galley and Chater from their homes, coupled with the fact that about the time of their departure Galley's greatcoat was found in the road very bloody, gave rise to suspicions that they had fallen into the hands of the smugglers and had met with foul play, particularly as the horse which had been ridden by Chater was found without his rider.

'These suspicions having been laid before the Commissioners of the Customs, and by them before His Majesty in council, a proclamation was issued, offering a reward to anyone who should discover what had become of them, and His Majesty's pardon to the informer. Six or eight months, however, passed before any light was thrown upon the affair, the facts of which were gradually uncovered by the following means:

'A person who had been witness to some of the transactions of this bloody tragedy, and knew of the death of either Galley or Chater, and where one was buried, sent an anonymous letter to a person of distinction, stating that he thought that the body of one of the men that were missing, and who were mentioned in Her Majesty's proclamation, was buried in the sand at a certain place near Rake. Some persons went in search, and the body of Galley was found, in an almost upright position with his hands over his eyes, leading to the supposition that he was not dead when he was buried.

'This discovery being made, another letter was sent, in which it was stated that one William Steele, otherwise Hardware, was concerned in the murder of the man whose body was found buried in the sand, and mention being made where he might be found, he was taken into custody, when he offered himself as king's evidence, and made a full confession of the whole transaction, and gave the names of the persons concerned therein.

'Steele's confession led to the discovery of Chater's body in Harris's Well, and to warrants being issued for the apprehension of the principal actors in the murders, some of whom were soon afterwards taken. John Race, who was concerned in the beginning of the affair at Rowland's Castle, came and voluntarily surrendered himself, and was admitted as king's evidence, as Steele had been.

'Hammond was taken in the beginning of October; and it appearing by undeniable evidence that he was concerned in the murder of Chater, and had thrown him into the said well near Harting, in the county of Sussex, he was committed to Horsham goal, on the 10th of the same month. John Cobby was likewise apprehended, and on 18th October was committed to Horsham gaol for the same crime.'

Matters Come To A Climax

'The smugglers had reigned a long time uncontrolled largely because the officers of the Customs were too few to encounter them. They rode in troops to the sea-side to fetch their goods, and carried them off in triumph by daylight; and so audacious did they grow at the last that they were not afraid of regular troops, that were sent into the country to keep them in awe. If any one of them happened to be taken, and even if the proof against him was irrefutable, no magistrate in the county durst commit him to gaol; if he did, he was not sure that his house or barns would not be set on fire, or some other terrible mischief done to him; as for anyone who informed against them or who in any way interfered with their unlawful occupation, a certain and terrible fate awaited him: the terrible menaces which they uttered against any person who should presume to interrupt them in their contraband trade so terrified the people everywhere, that scarce anybody dared to look at them as they passed through the towns and villages in open daylight.

'And the custom-house officers were so intimidated that scarce any of them had courage enough to go upon their duty. Some they knew had already been sent to France, and others killed or wounded in opposing them – so that Government at length began to be alarmed, and to apprehend consequences fatal to the public peace unless a speedy check was not put upon their audacious proceedings.'

The Goudhurst Band Of Militia

'The doings of the Hawkhurst Gang, however, brought matters to a climax, and the people of Goudhurst, in Kent, finding their lives and property unsafe, drew up a paper in which they expressed their abhorrence of the conduct of the smugglers, and their determination to oppose them. A considerable number of them formed themselves into a band called the Goudhurst Band of Militia, and they placed themselves under the command of a young man of the name of Sturt, a native of Goudhurst who had served in a regiment of foot, and who had been a prime mover in the formation of this band. The smugglers soon learnt of this confederacy, and contrived to waylay one of the militia, and by confinement and threats, extorted from him a full disclosure of the plans and intentions of his colleagues.

'After swearing him not to take up arms against them, they let him go, desiring him to inform his confederates that they would come on a certain day, attack the town, murder every one therein, and burn it to the ground. Sturt on this intelligence convened his little band, and took every precaution in his power to give the smugglers a warm reception. Some were sent to collect fire-arms, others to cast bullets and make cartridges, and every means were taken for resistance and defence which time and opportunity afforded. True to their threat the smugglers made their appearance, headed by one Thomas Kingsmill, who subsequently headed the gang in their attack on the Custom-house at Poole, and after some horrid threats and imprecations, commenced the attack by a general discharge of fire-arms, which was promptly and effectually replied to by the militia, by which one of the smugglers was shot. However, it was not till two more of them had lost their lives and many of them had been wounded, that they quitted the field of battle; they were pursued by the militia, and some of them taken and executed.

'The murder of Galley and Chater as before related, together with other doings of the smugglers, and the names of the most desperate of the gang – particularly of those who broke open the custom-house – having been made known to the king, His Majesty issued a proclamation with lists of their several names, declaring that unless they surrendered themselves on a day appointed, they should be outlawed and out of the protection of the laws of their country. He also promised a reward of £500 for the apprehension of any one of them who should be taken and convicted in pursuance thereof.

Goudhurst church

'This had the desired effect. Many were soon taken, and lodged in the gaols; and were subsequently tried and executed. Before, however, narrating the few particulars of their trials, I shall proceed to narrate another diabolical murder of an innocent man by two principals and two accessories, all of them smugglers and connected with the Hawkhurst Gang.'

Another Diabolical Murder

'John Mills, alias Smoker, son of old Richard Mills, after the execution of his father met with one Richard Hawkins, a labourer, who happened to be thrashing in a barn at Yapton near which the smugglers had concealed some tea, and accused him of stealing a bag which they missed, but which in their hurry they had in fact overlooked. Hawkins denying any knowledge of it, Mills nevertheless compelled him to ride behind him to a public-house called the Dog and Partridge, on Slindon Common, where being joined by one Richard Roland (alias Robb), Jerry Curtis and Thomas Winter (alias Coachman), Mills and Roland whipped the poor fellow till they were out of breath; they then stripped off their clothes to their shirts, and kept whipping him with their heavy riding-whips till they were tired of the brutal exercise. Mills and Curtis leaving to fetch two other persons whom they threatened they would serve in the same manner, Robb and Winter placed Hawkins in a chair by the

90

fire, where he died. They afterwards laid the body on a horse, and carried it to Parham Park, about twelve miles from Slindon Common; and tying large stones to it, sunk it in a pond, where it was some time afterwards found.

'Seven of the notorious villains having been apprehended by the vigilance of the Government, the noblemen and gentlemen of the County of Sussex, desirous to make public examples of such heinous offenders, and to terrify others from committing such horrible crimes, requested His Majesty to grant a special commission to hold an assize on purpose to try them; and they represented that as Chichester was a city large enough to accommodate the judges and all their train, and as it was likewise contiguous to the places where the murders were committed, they judged it to be the properest place for the assize to be held. Accordingly a commission passed the seals, to hold a special assize there on the 16th day of January 1748–9.'

A Special Assizes

'On Monday the 9th January, Jackson and Carter were conveyed from Newgate, and Richard Mills, junior, from the new gaol in Surrey, under a strong guard to Horsham, on their way to Chichester. When they came to Horsham, Richard Mills, senior, Benjamin Tapner, John Hammond, John Cobby and William Combleach, were all put in a waggon and conveyed thence, with the others under the same guard, to Chichester, where they arrived on Friday the 13th of January.

'The Judges set out from London on Friday the 25th of January and arrived at the Duke of Richmond's house at Godalming, Surrey, on the same evening. The next day they set out for Chichester, and were met at Midhurst by the Duke of Richmond, who entertained them at his hunting house near Charlton; after which they proceeded to Chichester where they arrived about five o'clock the same evening.

'On Sunday morning, the Judges, attended by the mayor and aldermen of the city, attended divine service in the Cathedral where an excellent sermon was preached, suitable to the occasion, by the Reverend Mr Ashburnham, Dean of Chichester.

'At the appointed time, the Judges – the Honourable Sir Michael Foster, knight, one of the Judges of H.M. Court of King's Bench; the Honourable Edward Clive, Esq., one of the barons of H.M. Court of Exchequer; and the Honourable Sir Thomas Birch, knight, one of the Judges of H.M. Court of Common Pleas – opened the assize in due form, at the Guildhall. Two bills in indictment were preferred, one for the murder of William Galley, and the other for the murder of Daniel Chater, to which the prisoners severally pleaded not guilty.'

The Gang Is Found Guilty

'After a trial which lasted till the 18th of January, and after hearing evidence of the most conclusive kind, the prisoners were found guilty, and the whole of them condemned to be hanged, which sentence, with one exception, was carried out on the next day at a place called the Broile, near Chichester, in the presence of a large concourse of spectators; the exception was in the case of William Jackson, who died the night before in prison.

'To give the sentence greater effect, their bodies were afterwards hung in chains. The body of William Carter was hung in chains in the Portsmouth Road, near Rake, in Sussex, and the body of Benjamin Tapner on Rook's Hill, near Chichester; and the bodies of John Cobby and John Hammond upon the sea coast near a place called Selsey Bill, in Sussex, where they are seen at a great distance both east and west.

'The bodies of the Mills, father and son, having neither friend nor relation to take them away, were thrown into a hole, dug for that purpose very near the gallows, into which was likewise thrown the body of Jackson. Just by is now erected a stone, having the following inscription, viz.:

"Near this place was buried the body of William Jackson, a proscribed smuggler who under a special commission of Oyer and Terminer, held at Chichester on the 16th day of January, 1748–9, was with William Carter, attainted for the murder of William Galley, a Custom-house officer; and who likewise was, together with Benjamin Tapner, John Cobby, John Hammond Richard Mills the Elder, and Richard Mills the Younger his son, attainted for the murder of Daniel Chater; but dying a few hours after sentence of death was Pronounced upon him, he thereby escaped the punishment which the heinousness of his complicated crimes deserved, and which was the next day most justly inflicted upon his accomplices. As a memorial of posterity, and a warning to this and succeeding generations this stone is erected, AD 1749."

'The stone was still there in the 1870s but has now disappeared. Two more of the gang were subsequently tried at East Grinstead, for murder, and executed – Henry Sheerman for that of Galley, and John Mills for that of Richard Hawkins of Yapton.

'Others of the smugglers were afterwards taken, tried, convicted and executed, some for being concerned in the murders of Galley, Chater and Richard Hawkins, and others for being present at the breaking open of the custom-house at Poole. Two among them, Kingsmill and Fairhall, were reckoned the most audacious and wicked amongst the smugglers: they were both tried at Newgate, and both ordered to be hung in chains. They both, Fairhall in particular, behaved most impudently on their trial, and were frequently reprimanded by the court, but to no purpose: Fairhall said "he did not value being hanged", and said before his trial, "Let's have a pipe and tobacco and a bottle of wine, for as I am not to live long, I may as well live well the short time I have to be in this world."

'When their sentence was known, and one Perin, a member of the gang, was ordered to be hanged and then buried, while Kingsmill and Fairhall were ordered to be hung in chains, Fairhall replied, in the presence of many people, to Perin, who was lamenting their cases, "We shall be hanging up in the sweet air, when you are rotting in your grave."

'They were hung at Tyburn, and the bodies of Kingsmill and Fairhall delivered to the Sheriff of the county of Kent; the body of Fairhall was hung up in chains on Horsendown Green, and that of Kingsmill on Goudhurst Gore, at which places they had lived.

Kingsmill, Fairall and Perin breaking into the Poole Custom House, September 1747, to recover their confiscated contraband

'The Hawkhurst Gang was thus broken up, and smuggling became a more dangerous proceeding; and since the public mind was fairly aroused by the atrocious proceedings of the smugglers, they took to highway robbery and housebreaking which ultimately brought many of them to the gallows. And so ended the notorious Hawkhurst Gang, the memory of which will probably never die out in this part of England. It is still not uncommon to hear middle-aged men say, "My grandfather told me this," or "I heard an old man say that". This gang was daring, desperate, cold-blooded and cruel. I have heard that going home early one morning, they met an old women, and one of the gang asked her how old she was; she replied, "Eighty-one." He immediately gave her a blow on the head with the butt end of a pistol, exclaiming "You have lived long enough!"

THE SMUGGLERS' RULE OF FEAR

'In the next forty-five years the daring of the smugglers grew, despite the authority's successes in bringing the Hawkhurst Gang to book. Large gangs of forty, fifty, and even one hundred, rode throughout the country, well armed with guns, bludgeons, and clubs, setting everyone at defiance and awing all the inhabitants. They established warehouses and vaults in many districts for the reception of their goods, and built large houses at Seacock's Heath, in Etchingham (built by the well known smuggler, Arthur Gray, and called Gray's Folly), at Pix Hill and the

93

The local shopkeeper was often the receiver of contraband

Four Throws Hawkhurst, at Goudhurst, and elsewhere, with the profits of their trade.

'Of the Hawkhurst Gang, twenty-two suffered the extreme penalty of the law for their misdeeds; many of the bodies were hung in chains, and this fact shows in a somewhat painful manner, the power, if not the majesty of the law. On the banks of the Thames, on salient points of the coast, particularly that of Sussex, these remnants were to be seen, placed there as a warning to those who might be disposed to resort to unlawful practices.' The story of the Hawkhurst Gang is the most detailed of all smuggling stories; less well known but of equal interest is the story, this time from Kent, of the Ransley Gang. The story is told by John English and comes from his book *Reminiscences of Old Folkestone Smugglers* published in 1885. As in the story of the Hawkhurst Gang the emphasis is on the wanton cruelty of the Ransleys, although the particular incidents mentioned sound suspiciously similar to those for which the Hawkhurst Gang was blamed.

THE RANSLEY GANG

'At Hythe, Old Ransley and his family, both men and women, were the leaders of a great body of smugglers who resided principally in the villages of Allington, Bilsington and Bonnington – villages through which the military canal from Hythe to Appledore passes, or very nearly approaches, and whose inhabitants, ostensibly agricultural labourers and small farmers, added to their little earnings by engaging in the hazardous trade of smuggling or assisting in smuggling by carrying away and circulating goods as soon as they were landed. Very few of them gained much by the work – only here and there one amassed money – and as a rule they eventually lost everything by engaging in an unlucky venture.

'The name of the gang still lingers in the locality, and strange and terrible traditions concerning their doings have been handed down. An old man, who has passed the allotted span of human life, but who still lives not far from Folkestone, is one of the few still left who actually remembers them. He knew the Ransleys when he was a mere child, for in his earliest years he was utilised by the smugglers as a sentinel, to warn the illicit traders of the approach of strangers while operations were being carried on. The scene of their exploits ranged from Sandgate to Dungeness, and in every town and village in the Marsh they had confederates and hiding places. In the later years of the existence of the gang, the members became more desperate. They were engaged constantly in deadly conflicts with revenue officers as well as with the dragoons who finally were employed to put a stop to smuggling.

'The old school refused to associate with them in their desperate undertakings. They saw no harm in "fair trading", but the cruelties which were practised were too revolting even for their unrefined and uneducated minds. The smugglers therefore became a sort of Robin Hood's band, although they lacked the gallantry of the bold foresters. Finally they grew so reckless and daring that they became a terror to the whole district. They would present themselves at a farm house, and demand whatever they thought fit, such as corn for their horses, and the like, just in the same way that the Scottish marauders used to do in the north of England. If what they required was not given, they took it.

'They even went to much greater lengths, and were guilty of acts of the most wanton cruelty. On one occasion, when returning from one of their expeditions, they came upon an old woman walking along the banks of the canal somewhere near Ruckinge bridge. They seized the poor old girl, stripped her stark naked, and then turned her adrift. When the foregoing appeared in the *Express*, an anonymous correspondent took exception to it, and contended that the smugglers would never have been guilty of such an act unless they suspected the old woman of being an informer. On this letter being shown to the old man who had reported it, he assured me that on one occasion a band of these ruffians met an old woman of nearly eighty years of age in a lonely lane, and one of them deliberately killed her by a blow from the butt end of a pistol, simply remarking that she had lived long enough.'

The smugglers' look-out tower at Hythe

The Gang Is Apprehended

'Owing to their many acts of wanton cruelty, the whole country became incensed against them, and at last a warrant was granted for the apprehension of the entire gang. One of them turned informer, and one night the whole of the leaders, with one exception, were taken whilst they were in bed. The one who escaped, my informant knew very well. His name was Tom Winder. He lived in a little old thatched house, and he managed to get out of a window and conceal himself on the thatch of his cottage while the officers were making their search, and so got clear. The others were tried, convicted, and transported for fourteen years.

The Walnut Tree Inn.

'It is a somewhat remarkable circumstance that the man who turned informer was convicted of sheep-stealing in less than a year from the time his companions left the country, and being sentenced to transportation, was sent to Australia to join them. The time rolled round, the men's term expired, and they most of them sent back to England for their wives and families, so that at the present time a large population in one of our most thriving colonies is the result of the transportation of the Ransley gang.'

So much for organised gangs; but there were also, of course, those spontaneous uprisings of large numbers of people determined either to rescue smuggled goods that had been confiscated by the authorities, or to effect the rescue of a local smuggler. This often got completely out of hand, as in the story which follows; again our chief informant is John English:

A Narrow Escape

'Lieutenant Peat was well known in Folkestone as one of the most strict of the officers engaged in suppressing smuggling. There is no doubt that many of them winked at the running of cargoes, if it was made worth their while. A seaman who served under Peat related to me the story of the murder of a quarter-master who was in Lieut Peat's company one night when he was set upon, and how miraculously the lieutenant himself escaped death. I do not know if this gallant officer is still living, but some years ago he was residing in North Britain, and had attained the rank of Admiral. The following account of the affair appeared a long time since in a publication called *The Battle and the Breeze*.

'At Romney, a smuggler named Walker had been convicted before one of the resident magistrates, who perceiving a disposition among the mob to effect a rescue, gave directions for the immediate removal of the prisoner to a king's vessel, then lying at anchor near Dungeness.

'Lieut David Peat, on whom this duty devolved, set off to execute his orders, accompanied by a magistrate, and attended by a slight guard of marines. On reaching the shore, the exasperation of the populace could no longer be restrained to oaths and execrations. Several stones were thrown, one of which struck the magistrate, who thereupon, as it is said, read a clause of the Riot Act, and commanded the mob to disperse. Instead of complying they attacked the cart, and dragged out the prisoner, at the same instant hurling a fresh body of stones at the lieutenant. Perceiving that in another moment the rescue would be complete, and that Walker was himself in the act of striking at the officer, the magistrate called out, "Secure your prisoner, sir. Run the rascal through!" The order was no sooner given than obeyed. Peat killed the smuggler with a single thrust. Irritated by blows and abuse Lieut Peat then surrendered himself into the hands of the magistrate, who returned with him to Romney to await the result of a coroner's inquest.'

The Coroner's Inquest

'The house in which the jury assembled was soon surrounded by a furious mob who kept shouting for vengeance upon "Peat the murderer!" It being evident therefore that some act of violence would be attempted in the event of the verdict exculpating the lieutenant, it became necessary to obtain protection from the soldiers stationed at Hythe – although there was great difficulty in despatching a messenger thither unobserved by the populace. At length, however, the magistrate's son contrived to steal out unnoticed, went to his father's stable, saddled a horse, galloped to Hythe, and delivered his dispatch to the commanding officer of the troops.

'Meanwhile the inquest proceeded amid a storm of vociferations. The coroner, being a man of firm and upright mind, charged the jury that Walker's death, under the circumstances detailed in the evidence, was clearly justifiable homicide, and after much reluctance and delay a verdict to that effect was pronounced. Hereupon the populace became perfectly outrageous, but at that instant a troop of dragoons galloped into the town, and the mob dispersing, Lieutenant Peat returned to his quarters at Dungeness without further molestation.

'At the funeral of the unfortunate Walker, fresh manifestations of enmity were evinced, and the inscription placed over his remains concluded with this quaint intimation:

By a base man my life I lost.

Overleaf: Smugglers Landing in a Storm by Philip James de Loutherbourg

'The brother officers of Lieut Peat, apprehensive that an attempt would be made to assassinate him, recommended his removal to some other part of the coast; however, with scant regard to threats, he not only resolved to maintain his ground, but plunged deeper into danger by coming to reside at Folkestone, where the whole population entertained feelings of bitter animosity against him.'

Lieut Peat Is Attacked

'The consequences were nearly such as had been anticipated. Going through some lonely marshes on a dark night, attended by a trusty quarter-master, Lieut Peat detected an ambuscade of armed smugglers, one of whom he fearlessly seized, when a volley was discharged, which killed the quarter-master and badly wounded the lieutenant. The latter, knowing that no mercy would be shown to him, had the presence of mind to feign death by lying motionless, when he overheard his assailants coolly discussing the question as to whether or not they should fire another volley at his body, one of them declaring that Peat had more lives than a cat, and would certainly recover if they did not make sure work.

'Thus urged, the smugglers deliberately reloaded their muskets, fired another volley at their prostrate enemy, and fled, leaving Lieut Peat still alive, but with fourteen gunshot wounds in different parts of his body. To the utter discomfiture of the free traders, however, the lieutenant recovered, was promoted and pensioned by the Admiralty, and astonished the inhabitants of Folkestone by appearing at the theatre attired in his commander's uniform.

'My informant told me that it was generally reported in Folkestone that three of the bullets were never extracted, and probably never would be.

[John English doesn't quite let Lieutenant Peat off scott free, and one anecdote at least allows the smugglers the upper hand:]

The Smugglers Win The Day

'After his removal from Folkestone, Peat took up his abode at Hastings, where he was superintendent of the coastguards. A cargo of goods had been landed a little to the eastward of Hastings, and worked up over the cliff with immense trouble, and under the very noses of the coastguardsmen. One of the officers was accompanied by a dog, the usual companion of his nightly rounds, and immediately over the spot where the smugglers were at work the animal halted and barked violently. The smugglers were waiting on a ledge of rock below for a favourable opportunity of getting to the summit. The officer, thinking the dog was barking at rabbits, called him off and rated him for barking. The smugglers laid still, and heard all that was going on, and after a while, when the coast was clear, they got their goods into a field, only a few yards from the superintendent's residence, where they not only rested with their cargo, but had the audacity to remain and refresh themselves with bread and cheese and beer – Peat himself even rode along the highway close to the hollow in which they were regaling themselves. His chagrin, when the affair became known, may be imagined. The owner of the dog and several of the men were removed in consequence.

'It was no uncommon thing for goods to be actually wrested from the revenue officers. The old custom-house at Folkestone, which is now used as offices by Messrs Henry and Co, was not a very strong place to withstand the attack of a desperate body of men and women, and several times it has witnessed a stiff fight. On one occasion, two men being imprisoned there, a terrific onslaught was made: the smugglers used brickbats, stones and other missiles, but the officers, armed with pistols, kept all at bay until assistance arrived to scatter the mob.

'I have also heard a story of a man who was proceeding with his horse and cart for the purpose of carrying away a load of spirits expected to be landed at a certain spot. The revenue officers, however, got scent of the affair, and as soon as the boat touched the shore they seized her. When the man came up with his horse and cart he was charged in the King's name to render assistance, and of course could not help himself. The cart was loaded with tubs of spirits and tea. Several of the "batsmen", however, hung about the spot, waiting for an opportunity to attempt a rescue. The driver presently caught sight of one of the smugglers peering from behind a hedge, and gave him a signal to follow. The party walked on quietly and unmolested until they came to a sharp bend in the road, where the "batsmen" had assembled; they immediately made a rush on the guards, and kept them at bay while the driver drove off at full speed, and carried the goods to their original destination. Of course he was well paid for his share in the transaction.'

Relics of smuggling days from Colchester castle (from l to r) lantern made out of an old whisky bottle; a case of hydrometers to test the strength of spirits; Custom House officer's pocket pistol, known as a 'barker' and a tinder box, or strike-a-light, in the form of a flint-lock pistol

TRICKS OF THE TRADE

To be successful the smuggler had above all things to be ingenious. This ingenuity might take the form of extraordinary hiding places – coffins, cupboards constructed up massive old chimneys, false keels or whatever – or remarkably well thought out double bluffs, deceptions and dummy runs.

DUST TO DUST...

Traditional respect for the dead and the convoluted ritual and ceremony involving burial was always an enormous temptation for the smuggler looking for a way to deceive the revenue man, as the following East Anglian tale, originally told by Athol Forbes, reveals.

There was to be a big run of brandy, silks, and lace – all the best stuff from France. A syndicate was formed, communication opened up with France, and the whole venture definitely arranged. Unfortunately with so many people engaged on the operation, secrecy was out of the question, especially when little crowds of men and women gathered on the shore to watch for the lugger. Coastguardsmen joined these little gatherings and learned all there was to know. One day, the long-expected French lugger was seen standing in for the Roadstead, and the greatest publicity was given that that was the ship. Coastguard and beachmen with their relations crowded down to receive a boat which had been lowered from the smuggler.

As soon as her keel grated on the shingle, the revenue officers and the fishermen dashed into the water and seized her. But here a surprise met everybody, because the boat contained merely a coffin, and the sorrowful rowers had a mournful tale to tell. The coffin contained their comrade, an Englishman who, in his last moments, had begged them to bury him in England. They were not smugglers, but honest traders, who simply wished to bury their dead and go away. True, England and France were at war, but the chivalrous English people did not make war on the dead; besides, their comrade was an Englishman. Excise and beachmen agreed: the dead man's wishes had to be respected. Sympathetic hands assisted the dead and the living out of the boat, and voices were uplifted in warm praise of the French captain's humanity.

Someone ran for the parson, others brought refreshments; everyone drank, but then all were mourners. The vicar arrived, and the sorrowful procession was marshalled by the clerk. The chief officer of the coastguard made himself chief mourner, and is reported to have shed tears; old enmities were freely forgiven in the general sadness. In the churchyard they stood with bowed heads while the vicar read the burial office; the grave was duly filled in and the crowd dispersed, to further the cause of international peace in the pubs and inns round about. But that night the grave was opened, and so was the coffin, and a smuggler's store received a valuable contribution in silks and laces – and laughter reigned instead of tears.

There was no suggestion that the vicar was a party to this proceeding, but it was not the first time that the church had assisted smuggling efforts. Finding something unusual or inno-cent-looking in which to hide a consignment of lace or a gallon or two of brandy must have given the smugglers an occasional headache, but generally speaking they were remarkably inventive. Athol Forbes, Henry Shore and the American Alpheus Hyatt Verril record the following instances of clever deceptions – only in these cases the smugglers were found out:

Hiding brandy casks
in a graveyard

ALL SORTS OF CONTAINERS

An officer of Customs noticed that old boilers used to pass frequently, from Poole and Hull to Ostend, and sometimes Antwerp and other places on the Continent, and he wondered why the same boilers should be carried to and fro as cargoes. One day he had a boilersmith take off one of the manholes, and when he had climbed into the structure, he found the reason in a ton of tobacco and 112lb of cigars.

This system of smuggling had been going on for years, and only came to an end in 1890. Some very influential people were mixed up in the business, although only one man took the blame and the punishment. Across the North Sea in all the seaport towns, there were at one time shops that catered specially for the smuggler. At Flushing there was a factory where tobacco was made up into ropes of all sizes; these, being slightly washed in rum, presented all the appearances of genuine hempen stuff. In 1842 at Portsmouth, tobacco was seized which had been cut into the shape of a man's shoe.

A Question Of Broomsticks

At about the same date customs officials became suspicious when they noticed a sudden increase in the number of wooden broomsticks being imported from across the channel. Vast numbers of the sticks came in, tied in great bundles, and the officials seriously wondered why anyone should bother importing articles of such small value, and which could just as well be made in Great Britain.

But it was no affair of theirs; labour, they thought, might be so much cheaper abroad that the broom-makers gained a few pennies by importing the sticks, and they soon dismissed the matter from their minds. Then one day two customs officers, chatting in their office, got to discussing the good old days; the conversation turned to the art of fence, and one mentioned the use of singlesticks. The other, who prided himself on a knowledge of fencing, suggested a friendly bout, and glancing around the room in search of staffs that would serve as dummy weapons, his eyes lit upon a bundle of recently arrived broomsticks. Here were just the things, and selecting two of the sticks, the men grasped them firmly and faced each other. But they were fated never to learn who was the champion because at the first blow and parry, the sticks broke like pipestems, and to the officers' amazement, a number of fine cigars came tumbling out! So the secret was revealed: each and every broom-handle was hollow, and was packed with the finest cigars!

An Unusual Haul For the Crabpots

Sometimes the smugglers tried straightforward bribery, and if that didn't work, quick thinking could make all the difference between success and failure, a fact revealed by a tale from Cornwall's Prussia Cove.

On a certain occasion, two Prussia Cove men were returning home from Roscoff in a

At the Custom House imported goods and luggage are searched thoroughly

small sailing boat well laden with contraband. The wind having dropped, they had been forced for the latter part of their crossing to labour at the oars and, thinking to save themselves the last few miles, decided to put in to Mullion. On arriving here, however, they found two excisemen waiting on the beach. Exhausted after their long and arduous passage, the smugglers offered five pounds in order to be allowed to land. Bribery in this case, however, proved of no avail, and so with heavy hearts they bent themselves once more to the task of rowing on to Prussia Cove. Meantime, the officers mounted their horses and kept pace with them along the cliffs.

Just short of the cove, the smugglers passed out of sight of the excisemen behind a headland, and here, much to their delight, they found a local man out in his boat, hauling crabpots. Making good use of their opportunity, they quickly exchanged the contents of their boat with that of their neighbour, and rowed on their way. They had hardly drawn into the cove before the officers arrived, and immediately set about a search – but in vain. It was not until some hours later, when the coast was once more clear, that an innocent-looking fisherman came into shore bringing with him a haul not often taken in crabpots.

A Convenient Confinement

A crafty move of an entirely different kind is recalled by the Cornishman Stanley Ord: 'On one occasion,' writes Mr Ord, 'a quantity of wines and spirits which had been landed on the coast near Padstow, was "warehoused" at a farm some three or four miles inland. By some means or other the excise officers had got wind of this, and in consequence a raid was expected. It happened, however, that just at this time the farmer's wife was anticipating a happy event, and accordingly the smugglers were seized with the idea of stowing the goods in one of the bedrooms of the house.

'Immediately after this had been done, the woman retired to bed and the doctor was sent for. Arriving before the search party, the latter at once took charge of the bedroom, into which he forbade the excisemen to enter on account of the critical condition of his patient. The remainder of the house, however, and the farm outbuildings, were thoroughly searched, but no dutiable goods being found, the party went away satisfied. Exactly how much of the contraband the doctor received for the part he had played is unknown!'

A Carboidful Of Spirits

Smugglers were famously generous in their gratitude for this sort of help – indeed, the fact that they spread their generosity so widely is one of the main reasons they could rely so heavily on local support. One elderly resident of St Just told the following story to the writer A.K. Hamilton Jenkin in about 1900, and it is recorded in slightly varying versions in a one or two other old books and newspapers:

'The night my youngest sister was born, I can remember we were all sitting up late in the kitchen, and about one o'clock in the morning a knock came to the door. Father got up to open it and found several men standing outside. "What's up, here, this time of night?" they asked, pointing to the lights in the windows.

'Father explained that a baby was expected. "Well," said the smugglers, – for such they were – "will 'e 'ave a drop of spirits to cheer yourselves up? If so bring out a bottle and we'll fill 'un for 'ee."

Boat Cove Skipway, Portheras Cove, St Just

'Father came in and started looking for a bottle, but not one could be found. The only thing he could lay hands on was one of those great glass carboids, like they use for bringing acid to the mines – an enormous thing.

'"Will this do?" asked father, taking it to the door. "Aais, all right, my dear," replied the men – though they must have been a bit surprised at its size. However, they filled it all the same, and then father gave them leave to put a few kegs in his barn, which was what they wanted. I was a small boy then, but I remember the night clearly enough, and I've got the carboid in the house still, though it's never been filled since!'

Stories like this are, of course, told in many parts of Cornwall. Similarly there are numerous wonderful tales of farmers, beadles, postboys and many others arranging their own patch in such a way that, in a smuggling emergency, a neat hidey-hole was always to hand.

A Gate-Postful Of Brandy

Adjoining a certain farm in the Padstow district there is a narrow lane which takes its winding course down to the shores of the neighbouring bay. On one occasion a local farmer was carrying a keg of brandy through this lane when he was spotted from some distance off by an exciseman. The latter, who was on horseback, galloped towards the farmer and fired his pistol as he went, in order to attract attention. Hurrying along the lane, the farmer dropped his load at a certain spot, removed a gate-post from its socket, deposited the keg therein and replaced the post, in time to greet the officer as he rode up with a cheery 'Good day'. In answer to the exciseman's question, the farmer denied all knowledge of the keg, and although the officer was sure that he had seen him carrying it, a search revealed nothing!

Another elderly Cornishman, Mr J. C. Hoare of Madron, who was still alive at the turn of this century, handed another story on to Mr Hamilton Jenkin:

The Shoemaker's Sideline

'My father, at the age of fourteen, was bound apprentice for the term of seven years to a certain well known shoemaker in the village in which he lived. The fee required for such an apprenticeship was ten pounds, a great sum of money for poor people in those days, but in return, the shoemaker was required to teach the apprentice his trade, to feed, clothe, lodge him, and pay him six pence a week, rising to two shillings by the end of his time.

'My father had good food whilst he was thus apprenticed, but the hours were long – from 7am to 8pm, ordinarily, but on some occasions much longer. The only recognised holidays were Christmas Day, Boxing Day, Feast Monday and Good Friday, with sometimes a half-day at Truro Whitsun Fair and Summercourt Fair. To vary the monotony of work, however, they often turned out for a night's poaching, also going to Gorran or Portloe, ten miles away, to fetch home smuggled goods – chiefly brandy. This latter was carried in small kegs, slung by a rope over the shoulders.

'On one occasion, when returning, they espied at some distance a party of excisemen, and were forced to take to hiding in a field of standing corn, where they remained all day beneath a hot sun, with nothing to eat or drink. On arriving home, the liquor they had smuggled was poured into a wash tray and coloured the right shade with burnt sugar, after which it was returned to the kegs and sold to trusty customers.'

The professional merchant seaman was also a master of the art – but like all serious smugglers he needed a good, reliable individual to take care of the goods once they were ashore. In this case that individual was a woman, and a most remarkable one at that. Her story was originally recorded by Henry Alton and Henry Holland in their book *The King's Customs*, published in 1910.

Tobacco Smuggling

'In the middle decades of the nineteenth century a great deal of tobacco was run ashore from the Pool of London by the sailors on board the packets and cargo-boats that plied between London and the Continent. The most daring and skilful dealers in this line were the sailors of the General Steam Navigation Company. Most of these men came from the neighbourhood of Folkestone, and were the descendants of incorrigible smugglers. A great part of the goods brought by them was conveyed ashore on the persons of professional carriers, and taken to the dwellings of professional receivers. The most famous receiver of all was Mother Gregson.

'She had a tobacco-dealer's licence, and kept a chandler's shop in Barking Churchyard, a shop which was practically a clearing-house for smuggled goods. She employed a number of lads (all under sixteen years of age and therefore immune from prosecution), who did nothing for a livelihood except carry tobacco ashore on their persons from the vessels lying in the Pool and at the London wharves, and tramp with it down to her shop.

'This juvenile smuggling force was known among the waterside folk as Mother Gregson's gang. Mother Gregson was in touch with many City tobacco merchants and shopkeepers. On one occasion a large quantity of tobacco was found at her shop. The goods were undoubtedly contraband, but she escaped by producing false invoices, which, it was said, she produced at a few hours' notice from some of the most respectable people in the tobacco trade.

'Some idea of the extent to which the conveying of tobacco on the person was carried on may be gleaned from the evidence of a waterside police expert of the time, who stated that "though 210 persons were convicted of this practice in 1842–43, it was his firm conviction that not more than one offender out of a hundred was detected". It should be borne in mind that a practised carrier could convey with ease from eight to twenty pounds of tobacco on his person (one man was caught carrying no less than 47 pounds). The crew of a Dutch vessel (ten in number) brought two tons of tobacco to London, concealed among the cargo on board. They carried this huge quantity ashore on their persons within a week, making several trips each day. It was believed that the customs officer who was employed to watch the vessel was bribed to turn a blind eye to proceedings.

'There was much smuggling of tobacco-stalks at this time too, the goods being used in the illicit manufacture of snuff. Many large manufacturers of snuff dabbled in this business. In 1844 a huge seizure of stalks was made in the Minories by several of the London police.

'The goods had been landed down the river, and thence conveyed to the premises of an eminent London firm, a firm whose name was a household word with snuff-takers. Flushing, Rotterdam, Antwerp, Hamburg, Bremen – these were places where much pain was devoted to the packing and manufacture of tobacco for smuggling into the United Kingdom, principally into London. The quiet and winding creeks and rivels of East Anglia had become favoured landing-places, the goods being afterwards taken to London in market-carts and carriers' vans.'

By the end of the nineteenth century, although many old inns and houses still contained physical evidence of the smugglers' trade, the lamps, kegs, baskets tins and boxes – many with false sides and bottoms – that had once been central to the trade had mostly been destroyed. However, from the papers and proceedings of a long-forgotten Scottish Geological Society comes one detailed – and therefore rare – account of a smugglers' box. The writer, T.V. Holmes, begins with a general attack on foolish differences between Scottish and English law:

SMUGGLING BETWEEN ENGLAND AND SCOTLAND

'Since the failure of the insurrection of 1745, successive governments have practically endeavoured to keep alive a law-breaking spirit by the creation of smuggling between England and Scotland.

'This almost incredible piece of folly had been achieved by the exaction of very different amounts of excise duty on certain commodities north and south of the Border, and was bearing evil fruit when Sir Walter Scott denounced it in 1825. But I found on talking over the matter with some members of the Association, that they were inclined to be more or less sceptical as to the former existence of smuggling between England and Scotland, thinking either that I had somehow mistaken Sir Walter Scott, or that Sir Walter had taken a romancer's license. And I could point to no writer who had treated of the subject but the great novelist.'

The Smugglers' Box

'Feeling the desirability of obtaining corroborative evidence, I called on an aged and respected citizen of Carlisle, who was also an old friend of my own, knowing that he would be able to aid me in some way. After some talk on the subject he produced a box, which he kindly gave me, and which he said had been used in smuggling about the year 1842. It is a

Mother Gregson ran her tobacco smuggling business with a number of young runners. As is common today, children are valued for the air of innocence they portray

square wooden box, about 9 inches long by 7 inches broad, externally, and about 7in deep. The lid is fastened down by four screws, and would consequently take some little time to open, a work that could have been done only with care and deliberation. Inside the box is a small keg, capable of holding half a gallon of whiskey. The space between the exterior of the keg and the lid of the box was filled with small pebbles, which alone would be visible on the partial loosening of one or more of the screws. While, if merely seized and shaken by an exciseman, no sound would be heard but the rattling of the pebbles. And we can hardly doubt that to the revenue official of fifty or sixty years ago, a collector of stones must have seemed a necessarily harmless if somewhat feckless person, incapable of anything so manly as smuggling whisky. This barrel, I am informed, never held anything but whisky at nine shillings per gallon, the duty being ten shillings. My friend's name I do not give, lest some slur should seem to attach to it in the eyes of a younger generation of Cumbrians, to whom opportunities of amateur smuggling are unknown, except on the occasion of a visit to the continent.

'From some notes which he copied from his notebook and sent to me after I had left Carlisle, I learned that salt, as well as whisky, had at one time been subject to a much higher excise duty in England than in Scotland. In the year 1822 a man named Harding, of Great Corby, was shot by an exciseman named Forster, while endeavouring to smuggle three stones of salt in order to cure his pig; an incident which may have had some influence in causing the great reduction of the salt duty in 1823.'

Perhaps in few matters has necessity more often been the mother of invention than in smuggling. To turn for a moment to south-eastern England: in a letter to the *Hastings Observer* dated 1 November 1880 and headed 'Reminiscences of Old Times', R. E. Wenham relates that between 1820 and 1830 smugglers at Hastings were detected in one case landing kegs of spirits hidden in what were apparently blocks of sandstone; while in another instance kegs were concealed in lumps of chalk.

Old houses and inns were frequently riddled with passageways and hidden rooms and cupboards, for the smuggling era lasted several centuries and there was therefore plenty of time for the slow evolution of the business: whole houses were sometimes built from scratch with the needs of the smugglers in mind. In Scotland, houses were occasionally discovered to have two cellars – one built beneath the apparent earthen floor of the other. In the south the smuggler builders were equally ingenious, as local author and historian John Banks recalled at the end of the nineteenth century:

THE SMUGGLERS' HOUSE

'Hastings in its smuggling days had a great many ancient houses. Some of these were well adapted in their internal arrangements for the concealment of smuggled goods. They were also very picturesque in appearance; there are still some remaining in High Street and All Saints Street. One was – and is – situated in Bourne Passage, and was once inhabited by a

The Smugglers *by Henry Parker Penlee*

man named Ben Butchers, who was dog-whipper in St Clement's Church. A dog-whipper was one who walked about the church in service time, with a cane in his hand, to

> "Whack the little boys
> Who in church-time made a noise."

'The house to which I wish to draw particular attention, because in it I passed some years of my boyish life, and saw during those years many incidents connected with smuggling, stood on the left hand. My father was a blacksmith, an excellent workman, and who, while he worked, worked hard, and when he drank, drank hard; nevertheless with that drawback he was a good father, for he took care that all his children should have as good an education as could be got in the schools of the day. He wanted no School-Board to spur him on in keeping his children to school, and he would have been a sharp boy who could have absented himself from school surreptitiously for a single half-day without my father soon finding him out.

'My father supplemented his earnings, as indeed most working men did at that time, by going "looking out," ie waiting for the arrival of a smuggler's boat and goods, and assisting in conveying them to a place of safety.

'The house had been previously occupied by a man largely implicated in smuggling transactions, and it was well adapted for the stowage of quantities of goods. It was old-fashioned. On the ground floor in the kitchen there was a large oven, not used for its legitimate purposes, but frequently full of smuggled goods; in one of the bedrooms was a large closet very often put to the same use, and in the back yard was an unused pig-stye, beneath the sleeping part of which was a large excavation which had been made specially for the purpose of concealing casks of spirits.

'Such was the confidence in each other possessed by the smugglers, that they never hesitated in taking refuge, and even depositing their goods in the house or on the premises of any of their party, even if the person were not engaged in the particular transaction. One night, a company being hard pressed, deposited in this house not less than from eighty to one hundred casks of spirits. I am not positively sure that my father had anything to do in running this particular cargo; I think not, as I recollect his being in a great passion on the following day, in consequence of the goods being there.

'Unfortunately one of the casks had sprung a leak, and there was a smell of brandy in the court. To make the matter still more dangerous, a coast-blockade man made enquiries, who and what was that man who lived in that old house. What the information was I never heard. No doubt the matter reached the ears of the owner, and determined him to prompt action, for the very next night my mother came and roused me up, about eleven o'clock, with, "Come, John, get up and dress yourself directly, and put on your Sunday boots." John did get up, and dressed himself, but did not put on his Sunday boots. He was wanted to assist in carrying the goods away. There were four or five men, my mother and I, making frequent journeys to a shop not far off, and the goods were all taken away in a comparatively short time. I soon learnt why I was told to put on my Sunday boots – it was that my footsteps should not be heard in passing along the street, my Sunday boots not being nailed, whilst my week-day boots had hobnails in them.

'As we had to pass close by the back door of an exciseman's house, silence was necessary. I recollect that my mother and I carried one cask covered with clothes in a clothes-basket each journey. I can well remember the floor of the work-shop to which the goods were taken, and what a curious sight it was in the dim light of a single candle. The owner expressed a grim satisfaction when the affair was over.'

A Port In A Storm

'Another incident took place in the same house which showed the confidence of the smugglers. One night my mother was staying up rather late, being employed in ironing, and I was staying up too, reading, when we heard reports of fire-arms in the direction of the Marine Parade. In a few minutes there was a great noise of persons running through the court. Our door was quickly and quietly opened by some of the party, and in rushed two or three men, each carrying two casks of spirits slung over his shoulder. In a moment they put out the light, and locked the door.

'"Don't be frightened, Missus," said one of the men, "but keep perfectly still." After a short time the noise of people running gradually subsided, and the streets became quiet. A cargo of goods had come in at the eastern end of the Parade, but the coast-blockade coming up unexpectedly, the boat had to be pushed off, and the few of the company who had loaded themselves had to run for it. Seeing the light through the keyhole, the men, knowing that my father frequently assisted in running smuggled goods, did not hesitate to come in as stated.

'"Any port in a storm," says the adage, and no doubt these men thought this a safe port, as indeed it turned out to be. After everything outside had been quiet for some little time, the men told my mother to relight the candle, and then they asked for a gimlet. One was soon produced, and one of the men bored a hole in the side of one of the casks. Setting it on one head, and pressing it on the other, he squeezed out about a pint of spirits into a jug, and gave it to my mother, with "There, Missus, that's for you." They then shouldered the kegs and took their departure with a hearty "good night," and we heard nothing more of them.'

A Lesson In Hydrostatics

'It was in this old house that I took my first lesson in hydrostatics; the spirits brought over by the smugglers were always over proof, and I can well recollect large quantities being put into an earthenware pan, and diluted with water till reduced to the proper strength which was shown by floating glass beads properly numbered; it was my part to watch them and see when the properly numbered one came to the surface.'

Rats, Mice And Bed Bugs!

'There were other occupants of this house besides my father and mother and we seven boys and girls – there was a large colony of rats and mice, and the old walls were infested with swarms of bed bugs. Indeed, so numerous were the last-named creatures that, when the house was pulled down, a jolly old butcher, who lived opposite the Anchor Inn, in George Street, said he saw a long procession of them going along the street looking out for fresh quarters! Where they went to history has not recorded.'

THE PARSON'S DILEMMA

The same writer records a wonderful tale of the local parson finding a large stash of smuggled goods in his barn, evidence that – in a hurry – the smugglers really would take enormous risks knowing, as they did, that most local people would at least be reluctant to shop them:

'Not only did the smugglers take shelter and deposit their goods where they knew they would be safe, but they sometimes left their goods where a certain amount of risk had to be run. It was not, however, an unusual thing for farmers to leave certain gates unlocked, or to put the key of a barn, or even of a stable, if an extra horse should be wanted, where the smugglers knew where to find it, being well assured that, barring accidents, the horse would be returned, and there would be a tangible acknowledgement, in the shape of a keg left behind, of the farmer's good intentions.

'The following incident, related to me by two reverend gentlemen, quite independently of each other, will serve to show the seemingly unwarrantable liberties the smugglers sometimes took with other people's premises. Some years ago, an incumbent of Pevensey had made his chaise-house a depository of garden-tools and odds and ends. Going one morning into the chaise-house for something he wanted, he found to his surprise that he could not open the folding-doors opening into it from the stable. Being aged and somewhat infirm, and his gardener being out of the way, he was puzzled to know what to do; but after a while he managed to climb up by the rack and manger into the hay-loft over the stable.

'Looking down into the chaise-house, he saw to his surprise the cause of the obstruction: the place was almost filled with casks of smuggled spirits, which had been deposited there during the previous night by a party of smugglers. Returning to his house, the reverend gentleman was sorely puzzled to know what course to pursue. Loyalty to his king and country prompted him to go and inform the proper authorities; consideration for his parishioners and neighbours prompted him to say nothing. The smugglers, however, kept an eye upon the movements of the reverend gentleman during the day, intending if they saw him going in the direction towards the proper authorities, quietly to prevent his progress. He, however, came to the conclusion that he would sleep upon it, and take action on the morrow. Lucky for the smugglers that he did so, as it gave them an opportunity to remove the goods during the night.

'Going to the chaise-house next morning, he found that the casks of spirits were gone, with the exception of one, on which was tacked a piece of paper, with the following written upon it: "For our parson, with thanks for his kindness." '

St Margaret's Bay, the White Cliffs of Dover

SCALING THE CLIFFS

Skill, quick thinking and ingenuity were needed, and not just to escape the exciseman: natural obstacles sometimes proved equally difficult to overcome. John Banks again takes up the story:

'The mode by which smugglers got their goods up the cliffs near Hastings was very curious. So determined had the Coast-blockade become, that the usual mode of running the goods became attended with great dangers, and the smugglers had to accomplish, with skill and cunning, what they had formerly done by sheer courage.

'Not only were rope ladders used, but various tricks were put into practice to deceive the Coast-guard. I will first describe the ladders; these were made of stout rope, about the size of a scaffold cord, and the rungs or rounds were made of stout hazel or ash, and securely tied between the two ropes. The ladders were made in lengths of about forty feet, and were made fast at the top by being passed over a crow-bar driven into the ground. If a greater length than forty feet was required, two or more lengths were fastened together.

'They were lowered at a convenient spot near the top of the cliff when the Coast-guard were yet on the beach below, and by the time they were driven by the advancing tide to the top of the cliff, to get to which they would have to go a considerable distance, the smugglers were among the rocks at the foot of the cliff. There they would wait patiently till the appointed time for the loaded boat to come in, when the tubs would be quietly and leisurely placed in a place of safety beyond the reach of the tide.

'As soon as the guard was withdrawn from the top of the cliff, the ascent up the ladders commenced, and once on the top the goods were pretty soon conveyed away. The ladders had of course been left by the men in their descent. The ascent was sometimes perilous; I have been informed that on one occasion the crow-bar by which the ladder was held, was so much bent that it was a wonder the whole affair did not tumble down the cliff.

'On another occasion a sad accident happened to one of the men engaged in this kind of work. He had assisted in bringing the goods across the Channel, and was not, moreover, in a condition for hard work, in fact, he was very unwell. The rungs of the particular ladder used had been placed father apart than usual – ten inches was the usual space – on this occasion it was thirteen or fourteen inches. When nearing the top, what with cold and exposure, the man felt himself unable to hold on; he consequently let go and fell some twelve or fifteen feet, on to a ledge of rock, where he lay till daylight, when he was found by the Coast-guard and taken prisoner. He was detained a prisoner in bed, with a Coast-guard's man keeping watch over him. He at length threw himself on the Queen's mercy, and was set free. It may be mentioned to this man's honour that he never would divulge the names of his employers. He is still (October, 1872) living in Hastings (as indeed are several others who were concerned in this ladder business), but is a cripple, and will remain so till the end of his days. This affair took place in January 1851, and was the last of the kind. I may add that this man has made me a rope ladder about twelve or fifteen feet long.

'One danger attending the use of these ladders was, when they over-hung a projecting part of the cliff, a man with a pair or three tubs slung over his shoulders would find the upper part of his body thrown outwards and his feet inwards, but without being able to touch the face of the cliff with his toes: such parts were avoided as much as possible, and places chosen where the cliff sloped from ledge to ledge.

'One very curious way in which the smugglers outwitted the Coast-guard, was by haul-ing goods up the timbered hutch or outlet of the river Asten, that then existed a little to the eastward of Bopeep Tower. The goods having been previously sunk at a convenient spot not very far out to sea, and which spot could be again easily found by means well-known to sailors, a flat-bottomed boat would be quietly rowed in the dusk of the evening towards the spot. Two confederates would about the same time, by dint of perseverance and skill, evade the vigilance of the look-out Coast-guard man, and would descend the square portion of the hutch which was built up through the beach (a similar erection now exists westward of the same tower), and at the bottom of which huge gates were hung, which swung to and fro with the action of the tide.

'Once down, a cork at the end of a line would be floated out to sea, and would, in a short time, be found by the man in the boat. The goods (tubs of spirits) having been separated from the stones used in sinking them, would be fastened to the end of the line, and being of less specific gravity than the water, would be very easily drawn up the hutch.

'On one occasion, two men who were engaged in an operation of this kind, found themselves, as it were, caught in a trap. During the time that they were below, a Coastguardman came and stationed himself at the top, knocking his heels, and wishing the smugglers, no doubt, at the bottom of the sea. Of course all the time he stood there, our "free traders" were obliged to be as quiet as mice, and it being a cold frosty night, one may easily conceive their unenviable position. One of the men has told me that, on that night he "got the rheumatiz", which has clung to him ever since. The men subsequently got clear off, goods and all.'

Outwitting The Exciseman

Elaborate hoaxes played on the excisemen by the smugglers must always have been rare, occurring only when there was perhaps some personal vendetta between individuals. But there are a few stories which show how the tricks of the trade could be used to settle the eternal argument in smuggling communities, one which can best be summarised in the question, 'Who was top dog – the smuggler or the exciseman?' Given the popularity of the local smuggler, it is almost invariably he who wins, as in the following delightful story which is told by Athol Forbes:

'To revert to the lighter side. It was a great joke that skipper Leggatt played on riding officer Hacon. Smuggling had got the upper hand, and the Government of the day was determined to put it down. Hacon was a sharp man who had done such good work on the Cornish coast that his life was in danger, so he was transferred to Yarmouth.'

Hacon Throws Down The Gauntlett

'He was not lacking in courage or in resource. He walked coolly into the White Horse, and at the very headquarters and festive board of a celebrated gang announced his intention of putting down this illegal traffic with a firm hand. Whether he knew the character of the men he addressed in the snug of the White Horse is not known, but when he did know, he did not turn tail. He was a smart officer in days when smartness counted for much in the service of the Revenue.

' "You put down smuggling?" said Leggatt. "You? Oh, by the Lord Harry, you don't mean it ? "

' "I do," said Hacon. "I have put a stop to it in the West Country, and I'll see some of you laid by the heels before long."

' "I expect you made some prize-money?" remarked Leggatt.

' "I didn't do badly," was the reply, "and I shall make more."

' "Are you inclined to risk any of it in a friendly way? For if you are, I will lay my fifty guineas against yours that I will deliver a hundredweight of tobacco at your house, handed in at your own door before you get wind of it being in the town."

'The Excise officer was on his mettle. "I live in Yarmouth; there are a hundred ways into the town. The odds are not good enough." There was no reason why even a sportsman should expose himself to unnecessary risks of failure.

' "But I will bring the tobacco over the South Town Bridge."

' "You will?"

' "Yes," says Leggatt. "Under your very nose. Here's my money," and he produced his purse.

' "I'll meet you with mine tomorrow, here, in this room. But when do you propose to run the stuff? There must be a time limit, if I am to win my money or you are to win yours."

' "You cannot always reckon on wind and tide," replies Leggatt. "But I promise you to keep my word within a fortnight, beginning this day week. Time up at curfew." '

The Bargain Is Struck

'The bargain was concluded. They were sportsmen – keen, resourceful determined. It was very simple. Within fourteen days the tobacco was to be conveyed to his house, and it must come by way of South Town Bridge. All that was necessary was a strict watch. So thought Hacon. He had plenty of men at his command; the bridge was a narrow one; his commission empowered him to stop and search anyone, any vehicle – it was impossible for a pound of tobacco to pass, unless his men were fools. Some were, but he had men whom he could trust.

'Hacon straightway began a strict blockade. Two men stood on the Gorleston side, another couple on the Yarmouth end of the bridge. Hacon paraded between, and in his absence the lieutenant in command of the Revenue-cutter took charge, and he made a bet on his own account. The first, second, and third days passed without anything remarkable happening. The fourth day two men tried to get past carrying bundles on their heads. They were promptly seized and searched; nothing contraband was found. Next day and following days the same thing happened. Men passed in procession, each carrying a suspicious bundle; careful examination proved them innocent of any attempt to cheat the Revenue.

'More than half the allotted time had passed. But each day came the ridiculous procession; each man was subject to and passed the closest scrutiny, nor was the vigilance of Hacon and his men relaxed. Sunday was a day of truce, and they rested. Monday, 6 a.m., saw all precautions in force. Pretty girls talked to the Preventive men. Sailors invited them to "splice the main brace" at the nearest public-house, but the Revenue supervision withstood all the wiles of the enemy. Crowds assembled on and near the bridge; the excitement ran high. A fortnight was nearly out and not an ounce of contraband had passed. Yarmouth men looked happy, and Gorleston men looked gloomy. Their hero's guineas were as good as gone. During the last few days Hacon doubled his guards. Free drinks were offered to them

Gorleston, Norfolk, a favourite landing place for contraband

by friends and refused resolutely. There was nothing to call attention away from the bridge. Work had come to a standstill, fishing ceased, bloaters were scarce, herrings at a premium.'

The Foreign Schooner

'In the midst of the excitement a miserable little schooner, more like a yawl, put into the bay at Gorleston, flying a foreign flag upside down. Three men came ashore in a boat; only one man spoke English, and he had difficulty in making himself understood. But much uncouth gesture and shouting elicited the information that a man was very ill on the ship, and that they sought a doctor. The man of medicine was watching the fun at the bridge, but grumbling at missing the fun, went aboard. A man lay in a bunk raving and cursing in English, French, German and Dutch.

'When the doctor questioned him he sang or swore as the humour of the fit took him. It was a curious case, and might have been interesting, but the doctor was in a hurry. He prescribed a cooling powder, pocketed his fee, and recommended perfect quiet to the patient; he then climbed over the side again into the small boat which had brought him. The next day showed the Dutch flag half-mast on the little craft. Communication with the shore revealed the fact that the poor fellow, a native of these parts, had wished to be buried ashore. This information was given to the doctor. He replied that was the vicar's business.

'"Where was he to be found?" Why, at the bridge, watching the play and the result of the wager, for this was the last day. The sailormen took no interest in Hacon and Leggatt, they shook their heads and made signs for a grave in which to put their dead shipmate.

' "Oh, yes, bring him ashore, take him up to the church and we will see to that." The Dutchmen grunted their thanks and pulled back to their vessel. Meanwhile more preventive men were put on guard. The service at Corton and Lowestoft had been drawn upon so that all possible help was at hand if Leggatt at the last moment should spring a surprise upon them. Hacon was sure no contraband had passed so far, and even the friends of Leggatt gloomily admitted he was right.'

The Funeral Procession

'It was near sunset when the funeral procession arrived from the schooner, but everyone had gone to watch the proceedings on South Town Bridge. The curate appeared at the church at Gorleston, then it transpired that the deceased had expressly desired to be buried in Yarmouth, of which place he was a native. The curate, anxious to be back to the scene of the wager, said the poor fellow's wishes must be complied with, and he passed the procession on to Yarmouth. His reverence was going that way, and he went with them, to explain in good English what they wanted, marching at the head of the cortège. But no explanation was needed. People knew the doctor had been called away to a sick case on board ship, and that the man had subsequently died, and was to be buried in Yarmouth. It was another triumph to that side of the river; it was Yarmouth, not Gorleston, where he would lie.

' "Stand back; get the procession through; stand aside."

' " A few hours now will decide the wager." The betting was all in favour of Hacon.

' "Get the funeral out of the way." It was a mad indiscretion for Leggatt to tell the Excisemen the very bridge over which he would bring his contraband – there was no chance. This was the burden of conversation. Yarmouth men laughed, and said Gorleston had been done down. The time was up at curfew – eight o'clock. It was now after seven, and the matter was becoming a question of minutes. People began to shake hands with Hacon, and spoke of the Star Hotel as a fitting place to celebrate the victory.

' "Draw a cordon across the Gorleston end, no one must pass now."

'So he gave orders, and the Yarmouth men cheered. Their side had won easily, hurrah! Look at the town clock – five minutes more! The town clock strikes eight. Cheers for Hacon. Hacon raised his hat, and looked at his watch, and when he had replaced it he found a number of people gazing Yarmouth way. It was Leggatt; he came leisurely along smoking a clay pipe, and there was a faint cheer from the Gorleston men, and then silence.

The Exciseman Loses The Wager

'Leggatt shook hands with Hacon. "When will it be convenient to pay me my fifty guineas?" asked Leggatt.

' "The boot's on the other leg," smiled Hacon.

' "I know the tobacco is at your house," quietly remarked Leggatt. "The dead sailor who wished to be buried in Yarmouth – was..." But the news had spread – as news does – and a big cheer went up from Gorleston throats, wild yells rent the air, men and women danced for joy – of course on the Gorleston side of the river.

'"You go home and have a look at it – and keep the coffin as a small present from yours truly," roared Leggatt, laughing. Hacon's remarks we omit, the occasion required strong ones, and strong ones they were. The excisemen started off to the residence of their chief.

'It must be seen to be believed. Of course some people lost their temper, that is always the way. Yarmouth hurled insults at Gorleston, and Gorleston suitably replied. Leggatt drew off his people, and the clergy stood on the bridge for peace. Hacon went off accompanied by a sympathising crowd, and he and they sought consolation in the cup that cheers. And while they drank, Leggatt and his merry men landed the rest of the cargo of contraband from the schooner, and we may add all the crew spoke English.'

John English, in his *Reminiscences of Folkestone Smugglers* (1885) has a wonderful store of stories concerning local smugglers who were just too quick or clever for the lumbering exciseman:

NOT JUST A BEDRIDDEN WIFE

'A man named Phillips, who resided at Brookland, was well known as a receiver, and constant visits were paid to his premises by soldiers and others, but it was seldom that anything could be found. On one occasion he saw a party of horse soldiers approaching, and he fastened up his house in order that it might appear that the occupants were away. The searching party, after vainly knocking, decided to force an entrance, and the old man then threatened them with a pitchfork. Whilst they were coming up, however, he had contrived to secrete a couple of bags of tea, some kegs of brandy, and some light goods, such as silks, in the bed of his wife, who was bedridden. The attacking party judged from the old man's conduct that he had a lot of goods on the premises, and they instituted a vigilant search, but without finding much. They actually went to his wife's bedroom, but he begged them not to disturb the old lady, and they left her in peace, finally departing with what they had managed to discover.

'Two or three weeks elapsed before they paid the old man another visit, and in the meantime a big lot of contraband goods had been consigned to him. He saw the men coming one day, and resolved to put a bold face on the matter. Accordingly he went out to meet them, and invited them to walk in and partake of refreshment, producing a jar of brandy, with which they made free. Seeing the old man apparently quite at ease, they came to the conclusion that he had nothing worth seizing, and after they had a look round they departed, the old man laughing at them for their lost journey.

'At that very time, however, there was a large faggot stack standing a little distance from the house, in the centre of which about 200 kegs were snugly stowed away. The soldiers had actually thrust their swords into this stack, but as the outer walls were three or four faggots deep, they could not reach the tubs.

125

Tea In A Pigstye

'On another occasion a man on horseback was pursued by officers while he was conveying two bags of tea to be stowed in this old fellow's hiding places. He was seen approaching, and riding round the house he dropped his load without stopping, and rode on. When the pursuers came up, they found the occupier of the house apparently busy cleaning out his pigstye, and took no notice of him, but continued the chase after the horseman, whom they captured at Ashford but with nothing in his possession. The tea which he was carrying had been stowed away by the old fellow in the very pigstye which he seemed to be engaged in cleaning out.'

The Pig Leads His Mistress A Merry Dance...

'This pigstye business calls to mind a story of some revenue officers being outwitted by a woman. They had made up their minds to search a house near Radnor Street, where goods were supposed to be concealed. It had private communication with neighbouring houses, and intelligence of the intended search reached the occupants only a few minutes before the officers were expected. Plenty of willing hands, however, removed what goods there were there into safe quarters, and when the searching party presented themselves the door was opened to them by a woman who had evidently been exerting herself, as she was panting and blowing at a terrific rate. "Good morning, Missus, you seem out of breath this morning," was the greeting. She was ready with a reply, however, to the effect that the pig had got out of its stye, and had led her a rare chase before she could get him back again. What could they do but sympathise with the poor woman? But having made their search and found nothing, they knew pretty well that something other than the pig had put the old woman in such a state of commotion.'

Ingenious Hidey-Holes

'Before the Folkestone Improvement Act was passed, the site of Harbour Street was covered with buildings, and in *English History of Folkestone*, there is an illustration showing the Pent Stream running beneath the windows of the houses. It will be impossible for anyone who knew the place in those days to look at it without having many memories of the past awakened. But those who have only known the town since the march of improvement swept away those old buildings, when South Street was the highway to the harbour, will be able from the little sketch referred to, to form some idea of the change which has taken place. Many a snug hiding place for smuggled goods was brought to light. In one of the houses still standing in South Street there was a strange discovery, made a few years ago during some

A dozen miles from the open sea, Maldon has a strong seafaring tradition, and although its importance as a port is now negligible it still retains a strong nautical flavour. The beach leading to the town is seen at low tide and at sunset

repairs, when a large cavity like a chimney, extending the whole height of the building, was opened up, and from its peculiar contrivance there was no doubt as to the purpose for which it was intended.

'A cleverly constructed hiding place was found at a public house now known as the Oddfellows. An amusing incident happened quite recently, which shows how the houses in Radnor Street and that locality were once used. The tenant of a house there had a calf kept in an outhouse, which was quite safe and sound when he retired for the night. The next morning, however, when he went while it was yet twilight to take it out for the purpose of slaughtering it, the calf was missing. The man, we may be sure, was not a little astonished, but a closer examination of the place showed that the poor animal had only gone down one storey lower. Just beneath the spot where it had stood there was a long disused "tub-hole" which had been covered over by a large stone slab, resting on a wooden frame. The wood in the course of years had rotted, and it had given way during the night, the calf dropping thus into an old hiding place of the smugglers.

'Dover Street, and Fenchurch Street, once thickly populated by smugglers, would furnish an endless number of instances of contrivances for hiding smuggled goods. In one house near the bottom of the former street there was a short time ago, and probably it is still there, a cupboard standing in a recess. On opening the outer door only a shallow cupboard containing shelves presents itself, but this is a false back – the shelves hiding a cavity large enough to store an immense quantity of goods.'

Smuggling In East Anglia

If Folkestone and other south coast towns were well furnished with old houses filled with smugglers hiding places, the same is certainly true of those towns and villages that lie along the bleak East Anglian shore.

Corringham

All along the coast-line of Essex numerous aged inns exist, whose connection with the smuggling traffic in bygone times can hardly be doubted. The Bull, at Corringham, situated on the marsh lands which border Thames Haven, is one of these. The Bull is a very, very old house, for though the main part of its structure dates only from the seventeenth century, one gabled portion goes back a couple of hundred years earlier. A picturesque mixture of styles, the Bull Inn stands facing the church, whose early Norman tower is one of the architectural wonders of Essex. In olden times Corringham was a very desolate spot. Although the immediate vicinity of the village is fairly well wooded nowadays, the adjacent flats skirting the sweeping intricacies of Standford Creek are forbidding in aspect, their ramifications being a very Tom Tiddler's ground for contrabandists, and inversely a very difficult locality for combined action on the part of the revenue officers.

'Inter-communication with Corringham must have been exceedingly difficult in bygone centuries, for the place was so isolated that it is inconceivable that anyone would have wished to settle there by choice, unless as a hermit. As late as only ninety years ago but one road touched the place, and that must have been in a very ill-defined condition. Nevertheless, the church with its fourteenth-century body and its early Norman tower, gives mute evidence that the population around must at one time have been respectable in point of numbers. One cannot but think that, hemmed in by marsh lands as it still is, and with Standford Creek so conveniently available, the settlement was used largely as a secret "bumping ground" for contraband goods from very early times. The district was formerly a prolific breeding-ground for the fen ague, for which opium in large quantities was quite legitimately taken by adults and children, and when the night fog hung thick and the "hob-bie lanterns" moved over the marsh little did it matter whether French brandy or Dutch gin had paid duty so long as it was potent – and not very expensive.'

The Bull Inn at Corringham, Essex

Manningtree

'With Manningtree, nearly forty miles distant to the north-east, circumstances were decid-edly different. Manningtree was situated on a recognized trade waterway, doing much business in the coasting line, and would no doubt be closely watched by the gaugers. But even here smuggling was rife. The King's men could not be in force in half a dozen places at once, and it may be taken as a fact that certainly three-fourths of the coast-side population were more or less in sympathy with the other party. The very streets and lanes of the little town on the Stour seem to have been planned with an eye to the contraband trade. Cocklofts are said to have run through one house to another in succession, to facilitate escape from the revenue men, and sections of these overhead passages still remain in the more ancient buildings.'

A hut on the marshes at Manningtree

Harwich

'In the bar-parlours of numerous old inns in such towns as Harwich, the skippers congregate and spin their yarns. The tobacco they smoke may or may not be smuggled, but according to W. W. Jacobs, "It is well known all along the water-side that this greatly improves the flavour." These old shell-backs are well worth listening to: however prolix they wax, their conversation rarely becomes anaesthetic. Rum, their favourite tipple, is in demand, yet as one of them sagely remarked, he hadn't had more than would baptize a fairy. I heard one weather-beaten veteran call to the attendant damsel for "a drop of Nelson's blood, miss", and the order was understood and promptly executed.

'In the open streets and lanes of Harwich many features exist, which to the discerning eye bear obvious evidences of the former prosperity of the place as a maritime port; but more remain hidden in cupboards and back yards remote from the public gaze. More still exist of the old-time smuggling trade, though inaccessible to the curious. Unseen by the wayfarer, Harwich is literally honeycombed with subterranean passages and caverns, a labyrinth once used to great effect by evaders of the revenue, but now choked up and forgotten.'

English's *Reminiscences of Old Folkestone Smugglers* contains an excellent account of one aspect of smuggling – guinea smuggling – mentioned by very few other writers:

GUINEA SMUGGLING

'Of all the smuggling pursuits which most called for daring courage, I know of none that equalled the so-called guinea trade. Gold was once at a tremendous premium, guineas being bought up in this country for as much as twenty-seven shillings each, and then the margin of profit was so great that firms of high standing among bankers risked everything to engage in the trade. The gold was conveyed to Folkestone by all sorts of means, and when it arrived it was distributed among people who could be trusted to produce it at a given moment.

'It was my good fortune to hear many particulars of this traffic from the lips of one of the chief members of a hardy crew, whom I will describe as Mr Mute (by which designation he will be easily recognised by Old Folkestonians), who has for some time passed away, remembered not only by his exploits, but for his quiet, unostentatious charity.

'Let us imagine a dark night, flood tide running, the preliminaries of the trip previously arranged in council at the Sail Loft on the Stade, the purses (ie long leather bags for fitting the body) disposed, and a galley steals out with great caution to run the gauntlet of the gun-brigs and their row-boats, and heads away for France, not always escaping a salute of musket balls from the look-out vessels, but luckily the muskets were of the Brown Bess pattern, and range and trajectory were uncertain. Any of my readers who have resided for any length of time on this coast are aware how rapidly bad weather frequently springs up, and will be able to form some little estimate of the risks incurred by the bold guinea traders in an open boat, labouring frequently at the oars eight or ten hours without relief.

'But there were giants in those days, such as Poskett, Sam Farley, Higgins, and others. An honest old guinea trader, Will Baker, father of the worthy attendant on the bathing machines, with whom I had many an amusing yarn, told me that one dirty night he had turned in for a little rest previous to the hour fixed for a run across and found, on being called, his unmentionables missing from their accustomed place of deposit; his wife in her anxiety had hidden them, and no persuasion would induce her to produce them. Threats of going to sea *sans culottes* had no effect, and Baker had to remain, fearing the gibes of his comrades far more than the dangers of the voyage. "But they let me down light," said Baker, "for you see, I'd only been married a very little while." Baker was engaged some time afterwards, as he emphatically put it, "principally in the light goods trade", in a large open boat 40ft long, with an enormous lug sail requiring careful "nussing", as he expressed it. On one occasion starting from Dover, the wind being northerly, the master of the Dover steam packet consented to give the boat a tow out clear of the land, and was rewarded by the steamer being beaten into Calais by ten minutes, to the skipper's intense disgust.

'But to return to our guinea traders, Dunkirk has been reached, the precious freight (generally £30,000) delivered to the receiver, the tired-out crew are placed under a guard to rest before returning, both crew and guard having what may be called a good time together.'

Weighty Transactions

'Another episode recurs to me in connection with the guinea smuggling. I have already referred to the eminent firm of bullion dealers who were the prime movers in this business, and of the mode in which the shiners were stowed away in hiding places awaiting an opportunity to embark them.

'One night, the weather being favourable, and all being ready for starting for a row across the channel, one of these long galleys was run on to the beach at the east side of the east pier. At that time there was a huge bank of shingle at the base of the cliff, and one end of the galley rested on the crown of the bank, the other being afloat. The weight of the cargo was considerable, and there was no support in the centre of the galley. The strain broke her back, and it was necessary to procure another in which to make the journey. It was not long, however, before the golden cargo was shifted, and a sturdy crew rowed safely across the channel with it. It may seem incredible that all this could be done within a stone's throw of the custom house. The story was related to me by an old smuggler who actually saw the occurrence, and the explanation he gave to me was, "Oh, they (the officers) was squared; it warn't worth their while to interfere."

'On another occasion in the hurry to get away, one parcel of guineas was left on the beach, and on being discovered, the honest finders straightaway took it to the Mayor. Whether or no it was confiscated, or returned safely to those who consigned it, I am not able to say. The probability is that the latter was the case.'

A Clockful Of Guineas

'In 1803 a member of a very celebrated banking house commenced business in London, and entered very largely into the illegal exportation of money. There are some now living in Folkestone who can remember in their childhood having seen boxes of guineas stowed away in hiding places by their parents who were so fearful lest the revenue officers should get an inkling of it, that they kept their children close prisoners, so that they might not by any chance divulge. A very aged man said to me one day when we were gossiping over these matters, "Ah, many's the time I've seen our old clock case packed full of guineas", and it seems the old coffin clocks formed very convenient hiding places. I cannot find out, however, that any of these gold pieces ever stuck to the owners of the quaint old articles of furniture, nor indeed is there any record of riches gained by smuggling having been of much good.'

Old Tussy's Last Venture

'The case of Old Tussy occurs to my mind at the moment. Old Tussy's figure was familiar not very long ago. In his early life he was the captain and part owner of a smuggling cutter. As far as what was known as book larnin' was concerned, he was innocent of any knowledge of it whatever. Nevertheless he was a splendid sailor, and could navigate his ship, and pick a course on a chart with any man in existence. He was at one time in affluent circumstances, but one mishap after another befel him until he was reduced to a very low ebb. One who was engaged in the coast blockade has told me that he remembers Old Tussy's last venture. A boat with 40 tubs on board was seized by the revenue officers, and in this little venture Tussy had a fourth share. It was his last speculation, and afterwards he got a scanty living by hovelling, bumboating, or in some such way. He ended his days in the workhouse, where he had cast his anchor to wait while the tide of his life ebbed away.'

'Cocktail' Smuggling

English, who is a rich source of little-known smuggling lore, goes on to describe a particular kind of boat that seems to have been peculiar to the Folkestone area: the cocktail. This was the local name for the six-oared boats frequently used by Folkestone smugglers:

'A rather remarkable thing occurred the year my father went away. A lot of our six-oared cocktails, which were used for bringing in tubs of spirits that had been sunk half way across the channel, had been seized by the revenue officers on suspicion, but the smugglers kept on going to sea just the same in boats which had not been stopped, to gather up tubs that had been sunk. One night after they were gone, the officers determined to go out to see if they could not capture some of them with tubs aboard. The smugglers, however, had provided for such an emergency, and had given the women instructions to keep a strict watch on the officers, and if they started, to go at once and light a big fire on the Durlocks, where St Peter's Church now stands. This fire they would be able to see a long way off, and it would warn them, so that they might sink the tubs again. The women went to work quietly, and got together an immense lot of straw and light stuff. No sooner had the officers left, therefore, than a big fire was at once kindled. The officers who remained on shore were sorely discomfited, for they knew of course what would be the result of the signal. They rushed in all directions for help to put the fire out, and the result was a free fight, in which the women as usual got the best of it. The ruse was successful; the smugglers saw the beacon fire, and sinking their tubs again, came back empty.

'Cocktail smuggling did not survive very long after this event, because one after another the boats were seized, until there were none left.'

Overleaf: Smuggler of Folkestone *by Joseph Mallord William Turner*

The Woman's Role

'In all these smuggling transactions women took a very active part, either in keeping a look-out, in assisting to secrete the cargoes, or in disposing of the contraband goods. In the latter case the devices resorted to, to get the goods safely into the hands of dealers in them were very ingenious. At the beginning of this century there was a house in Radnor Street called the Three Mackerel. It has since changed its name and is now known as the Odd Fellows.

'It was a noted house for the revenue officer, but although these gentlemen were constantly hanging about, the spirits were often smuggled in, even in broad daylight. On one occasion, two young women, one of whom is still living, but no longer young, walked boldly in, dressed as laundresses, carrying between them a large clothes basket. In an adjoining room there were several custom-house officers, seeing whom, one of the women called out to the landlady, "We've brought your clothes, Ma'am", and the basket was quietly transferred into the custody of the landlady. Its contents, however, were a couple of kegs of spirits, snugly covered with newly washed linen.'

All Sorts Of Ingenious Devices...

'By means of false bottoms to the boats a lot of smuggling was at one time carried on, especially in Folkestone, but no sooner was the trick detected than every boat so fitted was seized and sawn in half! Nor was this confined to fishermen, for as late as 1831 a custom-house officer suspected a pleasure boat which was sailing up the Thames, gave chase to her, and after a run of 20 miles, overtook and boarded her at Blackwall. Under the floor he found a number of tin cases, full of contraband goods, the estimated value being about two thousand pounds.

'On another occasion a boat was caught unloading on the shore, and the blockade men made a rush to secure her. One of them succeeded in getting on board before she could be pushed off. The crew, however, were not to be taken by one man, who was compelled to accompany them to sea. A day or two afterwards his body floated ashore. His fellow officers alleged that he was murdered and thrown over, but the more charitably inclined concluded that he had jumped overboard and tried to swim ashore, but being encumbered by his clothes, was drowned in the attempt. He was but one of the many who lost their lives either on the side of the officers or the smugglers.

'Only eight years ago an incident occurred which shows that the old smuggling spirit has hardly died out even yet, and an attempt was made to land a cargo of tobacco, which, if lacking the boldness which characterised smuggling ventures in former days, at least displayed a considerable amount of ingenuity.

'On the 12th March, 1877, the chief officer of the coastguard at Hythe detained the *Wasp* and her crew, consisting of the master and his two sons, for smuggling. The *Wasp*, a small vessel of ten or twelve tons, had been run ashore at Hythe, where five bales of tobacco, weighing about 300lb each, were washed up at a spot to which, had they been thrown overboard from the *Wasp* as she was making for Hythe, they might, from the direction of the tide, be supposed to have come. Five bales of 56lb each were subsequently washed ashore at Sandgate. The crew had been observed throwing the bales overboard, some of which were washed up at Dymchurch.

'The master of a lugger reported to the Customs officers at Dover on the 13th of March, that while off Sandgate he had picked up thirteen bales of tobacco, which he duly produced and delivered up; and there is no doubt that these also formed a portion of the cargo of the *Wasp*. The master of the *Wasp* was prosecuted and fined £100, and in default of payment, was committed to prison, where he was detained for one year, his vessel being sold for the benefit of the Crown.'

Tobacco In The Fuel...

'Still more recently an ingenious device for smuggling purposes was discovered at Dover on board the Belgian mail steamer. It was found that the firemen were in the habit of concealing tobacco in blocks of the patent fuel used on board instead of the ordinary coal, these blocks being placed among the bulk of the fuel. In such cases it is almost impossible to discover the owners of the contraband goods, and the smugglers, so far as detection is concerned, remain masters of the situation.'

Tobacco In The Timber Load...

'The following method may, for aught I know, be considered antiquated by the watchful authorities and consigned to the traditions of Rip Van Winkle, but as an instance it is worth recording. Some few years before the Great War a timber-laden vessel was unloading its cargo on the wharf of a large East Anglian river-side town which shall be nameless. On the quay a solitary customs official, off duty, meditatively watched the process. The logs as they were raised by the crane dropped with rhythmical regularity upon the wharf. The operation went on for some time in a simple, even, and perfectly satisfactory manner. But something went wrong and the unexpected happened. One of the logs in transit swung round and bumped heavily against an obstacle, the end came off, and from a cavity tumbled a lot of tobacco. The rest happened quickly.

'The ruminating customs man, roused sharply from his lethargy, took his opportunity, and a whole bagful of interesting proceedings followed. I forget what the sentence was on the offenders, but it was adequate.'

Tobacco In The Person's Attire...

'I have been asked if I have ever personally seen a smuggler caught in the act. Well, yes, certainly, but under very modern and prosaic conditions. The scene is Parkeston Quay in pre-war days. One of the Royal Mail packets has arrived, and a short, very square-built

foreigner, a typical Dutchman, with pale traces of recent nausea upon his countenance, is being interrogated by an affable customs official. Between them is a deal table.

' "Have you anything to declare, sir?" asks the officer, and the usual formula follows.

' "Nein," answers the big man with the hunched-up shoulders.

'"Quite sure, sir?" queries the customs official.

'"Ja, ja."

' "Will you please take off your overcoat, sir," from the bland official, the faintest suggestion of an iron hand penetrating through the velvet-glove manner.

Protests in Dutch and broken English.

'"George," said the CHO quietly, "take off the gentleman's overcoat."

Voluble protests. Many packets of tobacco are disclosed. The lining of the great-coat reveals a perfect armoury of contraband.

'"Anything more, sir?" – blandly.

'"Nein."

'"Take off the gentleman's jacket, George."

'Order promptly obeyed. More disclosures of contraband packing.

I will cut short the narration. Disrobing proceeded, and the man was unpicked until he presented the spectacle of a narrow-shouldered, under-developed creature of insignificant, not to mention scowling appearance.

'"Anything more to declare, sir?"

'No answer.

'"Take off the gentleman's hat, George."

'Order obeyed. The headpiece, a square-topped bowler, was removed and a parcel of cigars fell out of it.'

Sharing a pipe of tobacco and a good yarn. Was the tobacco smuggled?

139

By the time English was writing this, smugglers were no longer the Robin Hood figures they had once been. The tide of history was turning against them, and it was time for a few battles to be won by the authorities, which brings us to English's last tale, in which quick thinking by a customs man brings defeat for the smugglers...

AN UNEXPECTED HAUL

'The system of using makeshift block and tackle to haul large tubs of contraband up the cliffs was resorted to occasionally. One very dark night a party of smugglers began to winch a cargo up the cliffs before the last customs sentinel had left the beach. The look-out man gave timely notice of his approach, and the whole party pushed off in their boat, unseen. In the confusion, however, they forgot to give the usual signal for pulling up the tub, which was left on the beach, and the sentinel coastguard stumbled over it. The men at the top began to haul away, and the sentinel jumped into the basket, being determined to find out what was going on. He actually held fast until he was landed at the top, when he immediately fired his pistol, and the smugglers made off, leaving the whole of the apparatus in the hands of the officer.'

CRIME & PUNISHMENT

When smugglers were caught in the act of running contraband goods, they were subject to two kinds of punishment. If they were seafaring people they were sent on board a Royal Navy man-of-war and made to serve for three, five or seven years – and given the state of the Navy at the time, a more brutal sentence it would be hard to imagine. If they were ordinary mortals they were sent to prison, and heavily fined. The gaols in most parts of the country were scarcely ever free from smugglers, and we read in periodical publications of the eighteenth century that the bodies of hanged smugglers were not infrequently displayed at crossroads hung in chains – a brutal business that was meant to serve as a warning to others.

By the end of the nineteenth century, most of those who wrote about smuggling either in books or the newspapers were doing their best to play down the popular image of the smuggler. They were keen to emphasise that he was, after all, just a common criminal, and at times a pretty ruthless one. John Banks, writing in 1871, is sometimes grudgingly sympathetic towards the smugglers, but he was aware that their character as latter-day Robin Hoods was exaggerated. Despite family connections with the trade, he clearly believed that, when caught, they deserved to be punished. Banks' ambivalent attitude is clear, too, in that when he describes a smuggler's escape from prison he seems to be saying 'Good luck' to him; in his own words:

'We must not forget that the smuggler of the last century was generally a lawless fellow, and did not scruple to add highway robbery, house-breaking, and even murder to his lawless pursuit of smuggling; and woe betide the poor wretch who should dare to give any information of his doings.'

A DARING ESCAPE

'Not unfrequently did smugglers escape. A friend of mine witnessed the escape of a smuggler from a hulk at Rye Harbour. This man had been confined on board the hulk preparatory to his being sent to sea. Watching his opportunity, he made his exit from his temporary prison; and, notwithstanding his being hotly pursued, he made his escape.

'There were, in the smuggling times of the nineteenth century, many curious and

141

daring incidents connected with the escapes of smugglers. A man, a native of Bexhill, a great part of whose life had been spent in smuggling, made two daring escapes – on one occasion he and others were taken prisoners, and were taken before the Mayor of Winchelsea. The Town Hall of Winchelsea stands in the north-west angle of one of the rectangular blocks of buildings of which that town is composed. The ground floor is occupied by the lock-up, and the floor above comprises the Hall. The door of the Hall does not communicate with the street, but is at the top of a flight of steps which are in a sort of court. The town clerk, a wise man in his day and generation, thinking to make all sure, as soon as the prisoners, the witnesses, and the public were in the Hall, and the mayor and other magistrates had taken their places on the bench, ordered the outer door, ie the door leading from the street into the court, to be locked, and the key to be deposited on the table in front of him.

'The weather being somewhat warm, and the place somewhat small and ill-ventilated, the windows were thrown open. I believe that there is no particular arrangement in the interior of this Hall for the placing of the prisoners in any particular position, so that our hero found but little difficulty in gradually getting near the window, as if for air. Without any warning he leapt from the window into the street; some of the Blockade looked out after him, but dared not fire, for fear of hitting some innocent person, there being a great many about in the street; some of them rushed out of the Hall, into the court; but found the gate locked! They returned for the key; but when they got the outer door unlocked, our smuggler was safe away. He, doubtless, knew every inch of the road he meant to take, and doubtless, also, had plenty of assistance from the onlookers.'

A Second Daring Escape

'The same man, with another, who was nicknamed Spinner, was taken prisoner, and was confined in Bopeep Tower. When smugglers were taken and in prison there was generally no difficulty in their friends obtaining permission to see them. This man's mother paid him a visit when he was thus in durance vile, and she managed to smuggle him a rope or line with which he succeeded in letting himself off the top of the Tower. The prisoners were allowed to take air and exercise on the top of the Tower, and on this occasion he fastened his line round the stove-pipe which came up through the roof, and let himself down over the parapet on to the beach. Once there, he walked leisurely to a public house about one hundred yards off, where a horse and cart were in waiting. The driver kept waving his hand to Spinner for him to come off the Tower in the same way, but he would not venture; so they were obliged to depart without him, and our smuggler again made good his escape. I have been informed that this bold smuggler is now living in a seaport in the West of England.'

The 'look-out' tower in Rye, East Susex (centre right of the photograph)

THE PROFITS OF SMUGGLING

But if smugglers risked long years in disease-infested prisons, what were the rewards? What made them risk so much? The answer for most smugglers was probably that successful smuggling meant the difference between a life lived at or near starvation levels and a life of relative opulence. And if life without smuggling was frequently pretty unbearable, then it was worth risking that life in an enterprise that could transform one's existence. John Banks is again our guide:

'To show the profit connected with smuggling, take for example a single tub of spirits; its cost in France was from ten shillings and sixpence to thirteen shillings – fourteen to sixteen shillings would be thought dear. A tub of spirits contained three and a half gallons of spirit so much over-proof that it would bear the addition of two and a half gallons of water, and the six gallons would sell easily for three or even four pounds or guineas. (Our forefathers had a great love for guineas.) Here was a profit of from four to five hundred per cent! After paying out of this the cost of transport, wages of the look-out men, etc the profits were so good, that I have heard it said that if one cargo out of three was saved, there was then a profit.'

In fact, as Banks explains, the profits – or at least the potential profits – were so great that just about everyone was tempted. A more enlightened age would have realised that the laws which imposed the taxes that led to smuggling in the first place should have been reformed, if for no other reason than that it was impossible to enforce them.

'One wonders now, in these days of enlightened fiscal legislation, how Governments could ever have been so stupid as to rest satisfied with a state of things so short-sighted. Even the Custom-house officers themselves smuggled, or at least sent for smuggled goods, and then gave information against, not themselves, but the cargo, for the purpose of receiving the Government allowance for seized goods, this being actually more than the original cost of the goods on the other side of the Channel. By 1816 the punishment for a smuggling had been carefully codified. Before that date magistrates imposed what sentences they liked, but the legislation of 1816 made matters far more straightforward. This read as follows:

The 1816 Legislation

'Every person found assisting in unshipping any goods may be arrested, and if convicted is to be committed to hard labour in the house of correction for any term not exceeding three years nor less than one year. If any person so convicted is approved of as fit to serve His Majesty, the justice shall adjudge him to serve as a soldier or a sailor for a term of five years.'

On the face of it the punishment sounds severe, but the smuggler still benefited from his popular image. The prison officials knew he was not a felon in the ordinary sense, though the law had condemned him, and they usually refused to regard him as a criminal. The Navy welcomed a useful man, and the boatswain who licked the raw recruits into shape did not like a man the less who, as one commentator puts it, 'had a spice of the devil in him and had defied the smuggling laws'.

Once on a man-o'-war, the smuggler's skills as a seaman would have made him valuable, and Lord Exmouth is reported to have said that the smugglers were among the pick of his ship's company. Steadily the new system of protection began to prevail over the 'free trade', and created new and subtler ways of cheating the Revenue. The stuff had to be handled in smaller quantities, so a lugger would run up the coast delivering small consignments to the various villages.

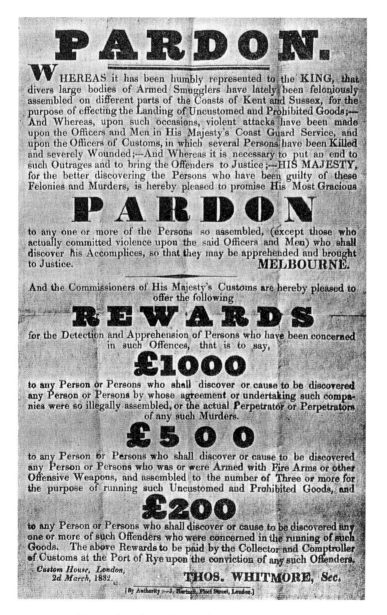

Notice of Pardon and Reward for Informers, 1832

The success of the smuggling trade entirely depended, of course, on the loyalty of all parties concerned, and true to the Cornish motto of 'One and All', it was rarely that this loyalty was ever betrayed. However, such betrayal did of course occur from time to time – for instance, in the village of Shuffley, near Redruth – formerly one of the greatest resorts of the smugglers in the tin-mining districts – one particular family was remembered well into this century as having produced an informer about three generations earlier. In many ways it is true to say that the informer who was caught suffered a harsher penalty than the convicted smuggler.

SOME CASES OF MISTAKEN IDENTITY

The crimes were not all on the side of the smugglers. Occasionally, and perhaps inevitably, the excisemen over-stepped the mark. In 1799, a couple of preventive men, travelling between Bodmin and Truro, fell in with two persons whom, for some reason or other, they suspected of carrying smuggled goods.

'This, however,' as a correspondent states in the *Gentleman's Magazine* for 27 June 1799, 'not being the case, the suspects put up an obdurate resistance, until at length being overpowered by their desperate antagonists they were left dead on the spot. The excisemen then absconded.'

Whether the Government took any action in the matter is now impossible to discover. Perhaps the outcome was similar to that in the case of the American judge of the pioneer days who, on finding that he had hanged an innocent man by mistake, is said to have apologised to the widow with the words: 'Gee, marm, I guess you've got the laugh over us this time.' Though this must have provided small consolation for the relatives of the unfortunate victims, there can be no doubt that keen satisfaction was felt by the countryside at large at such a discomfiture of the hated searchers. This, however, was not the only occasion on which the justice of the law miscarried with tragic results, as is revealed by the inscription on a tombstone, dated 1814, standing in the little churchyard of Mylor, near Falmouth:

> We have not a moment we can call our own.
> Officious zeal in luckless hour laid wait
> And wilful sent the murderous ball of Fate!
> James to his home, which late in health he left,
> Wounded returns – of life is soon bereft.

The memorial leaves little doubt of the strength of popular feeling which was aroused on this occasion, for in this case the victim of the excisemen's aggression was no stranger but a young man of the village: returning in his boat one evening after having been out fishing, was fired upon by the officers and fatally wounded. The smugglers themselves, however,

Boscastle Harbour from Penally Point

146

sometimes made mistakes, and since attacks upon the detested excisemen were generally made under cover of darkness, a hard fate occasionally awaited the individual who happened to look, ride or walk like an exciseman!

The following is a tale related by several authors: one night in the early part of the nineteenth century, a Truro gentleman was riding home from Redruth at a late hour, when he suddenly found himself surrounded by a band of smugglers, who shouted: 'Knack 'un down! Knack 'un down! and scat his head abroad 'pon the floor!' The gentleman, realising the mistake which had been made, quickly undeceived them, and at this the smugglers, in tones of deepest repentance, exclaimed: 'Arreah! why, 'tes Maister S– from ovver to Trura, why we wud'n hurt a heer of hes head.' Saying which they remounted Mr S– on his horse and escorted him far on his way home, finally taking leave of him with renewed apologies for the inconvenience which had been caused by his mistaken identity.

A Tale Of Being The Good Samaritan

Though they hated the excisemen for their interference in what was locally regarded as an honest trade, the Cornish people could be generous even to their enemies when in distress. During one bitterly cold and pitch-black night in December, 1805, two excise officers, travelling from Luxillian to Lostwithiel, lost their way, and after proceeding for several miles across country, at length found themselves in the desolate region of the Goss Moors. There they wandered for several hours, and at last became so exhausted that they sank down on the ground unable to proceed any farther. Fortunately for them, soon afterwards two smugglers on their way to their night's labour chanced to hear their groans, and immediately went to their relief, thereby in all probability saving them from death by exposure.

In smuggling – and indeed as in other of the more adventurous games of life – the strands of humour and tragedy, generosity and meanness, were closely interwoven.

A Joke Misinterpreted

From Scotland, while we are on the subject of humour, comes the following delightful tale, which was noted down by at least two writers of the time, including Athol Forbes:

'The leader of a band of smugglers married a simple lass from Inverness-shire. The contraband trade was something new to her, and when her husband came ashore and put into her hands a keg of very choice brandy, she asked what she was to do with it.

"Why, you might take it to Lieutenant Phillips," he laughed. But she took his joke seriously and obeyed it literally, and her husband was arrested. However, the circumstances were so remarkable that my grandfather released him, and the brandy was shared by smugglers and servicemen alike.

Any Victorian story of a life of crime followed by years of sincere repentance should be treated with suspicion since the Victorians loved to put this sort of spin on things. However, if we are prepared to take the ending with a pinch of salt, the following tale is a fascinating one as it purports to come, as it were, from the horse's mouth. Captain Harry Carter of Prussia Cove, Cornwall, certainly existed, and the story of his life, recorded at first hand by a number of authors, gives a vivid and convincing picture of the life of a smuggler. It was first published in 1894.

THE ADVENTURES OF CAPTAIN HARRY CARTER

'In the year of 19th April, 1786, I was married to Elizabeth Flindel, of Helford, in the parish of Manaccan, and in April 19, in 1787, she bore me a daughter, who was called after her mother's name, and I think it was aboute middle of November I went in a luggar, smuggling. She was 45 tons, mounting sixteen carriage guns. After making one voyage at home to the King's Cove I got a freight for Cawsand near Plymouth and as I depended on them people to look out if there were any danger according to their promise, came into the Bay, and after sume time spoke with a boate from the above place, saying it was a clear coast, there was no danger to bring the vessel up to anchor, and we should have boats enough out to dis-charge all the cargo immediately. So that I brought the vessel to anchor, leaving the jib with the trysail and mizen set, and begun to make ready, opening the hatches, etc. when I saw two boats rowing up from the shore. I said to the pilot, "There is two boats acoming". He answered, "They are our boats coming to take the goods out," etc.

'Soon after a boat come along side. "Do you know these is two man-o'-war's boats?" We immediately cutt the cable, and before the luggar gathered headway were right under the starn. They immediately cutt off the mizen sheet, and with a musket shot off the trysal tack and boarded us over the starn. My people having sume muskets, dropt them down and went below. I knowing nothing of that, thought that all would stand by me. I begun to engage them as well as I could without anything in my hands, as they took us in surprise so suddenly, I having my great coat on buttoned aboute me, I seeing none of my people, only one man at the helm; and when they saw no person to oppose them, turned upon me with their broad swords, and begun to beat away upon my head.

'I found the blows very heavey – crushed me down to the deck – and as I never loosed my senses, rambled forward. They still pursued me, beating and pushing me, so that I fell down on the deck on a small raft just out of their way. I suppose I might have been there aboute a quarter of an hour, until they had secured my people below, and after found me laying on the deck. One of them said, "Here is one of the poor fellows dead". Another made answer, "Put the man below". He answered again, saying, "What use is it to put a dead man below?" and so past on.

'Aboute this time the vessel struck aground, the wind being about east-south-east very hard, right on the shore. So there I laid very quiet for near the space of two hours, hearing their discourse as they walked by me, the night being very dark on the 30 Jan 1788.

'When some of them saw me lying there, said, "Here lays one of the fellows dead", one of them answered as before, "Put him below". Another said, "The man is dead". The com-manding officer gave orders for a lantern and candle to be brought, so they took up one of my legs, as I was lying upon my belly; he let it go, and it fell as dead down on the deck. He likewayse put his hand up under my clothes, between my shirt and my skin, and then examined my head, and so concluded, saying, "The man is so warm now as he was two hours back, but his head is all to atoms".

'I have thought hundreds of times since what a miracle it was I neither sneezed, coughed, nor drew breath that they perceived in all this time, I suppose not less than ten or fifteen minutes. The water being ebbing, the vessel making a great heel towards the shore, so that in the course of a very little time after, as their two boats was made fast alongside, one of them broke adrift. Immediately there was orders given to man the other boat in order to fetch her; so that when I saw them in the state of confusion, their gard broken, I thought it was my time to make my escape, so I crept on my belly on the deck, and got over a large raft just before the main mast, close by one of the men's heels, as he was standing there handing the trysail. When I got over the lee-side I thought I should be able to swim on shore in a stroke or two. I took hold of the pulleys or butins of the mast, and as I was lifting myself over the side, I was taken with the cramp in one of my thighs. So then I thought I should be drowned, but still willing to risk it, so that I let myself over the side very easily by a rope into the water, fearing my enemies would hear me and then let go.

'As I was very near the shore, I thought to swim onshore in the course of a stroke or two, as I used to swim so well, but soon found out my mistake. I was sinking almost like a stone, and hauling astarn in deeper water, when I gave up all hopes of life, and begun to swallow some water. I found a rope under my breast, so that I had not lost all my senses. I hauled upon it, and soon found one end fast to the side just where I went overboard, which gave me a little hope of life. So that when I got there, could not tell which was best, to call to the man-of-war's men to take me in, or to stay there and die, for my life and strength was allmost exhausted; but while I was thinking of this, touched bottom with my feet.

'Hope then sprung up, and I soon found another rope, leading towards the head of the vessel in shoaler water, so that I veered upon one and hauled upon the other that brought me under the bowsprit, and then at times, upon the sand of a sea, my feet was almost dry. I thought then I would soon be out of their way. Let go the rope, but as soon as I attempted to run, fell down, and as I fell, looking round about me, saw three men standing close by me. I know they were the man of-war's men seeing for the boat, so I lyed there quiet for some little time, and then creeped upon my belly I suppose about the distance of fifty yards; and as the ground was scuddy, some flat rock mixt with channels of sand, I saw before me a channel of white sand, and for fear to be seen creeping over it, which would take some time, not knowing there was anything the matter with me, made the second attempt to run, and fell in the same manner as before.

'My brother Charles being there, looking out for the vessel, desired some of Cawsand men to go down to see if they could pick up any of the men dead or alive, not expecting ever to see me any more, almost sure I was either shot or drowned. One of them saw me fall,

View of Mullion Cove showing harbour walls and island

ran to my assistance, and taking hold of me under the arm says, "Who are you?" So as I thought him to be an enemy, made no answer. He said, "Fear not, I am a friend; come with me." And by that time forth was two more come, which took me under both arms, and the other pushed me in the back, and so dragged me up to the town. I suppose it might have been about the distance of the fifth part of a mile.

'My strength was almost exhausted; my breath, nay, my life, was almost gone. They took me into a room where there were seven or eight of Cawsand men and my brother Charles, and when he saw me he knew me by my great coat, and cryed with joy, "This is my brother!" So then they immediately stript off my wet clothes, and one of them pulled off his shirt from off him and put on me, sent for a doctor, and put me to bed.

'Well, then, I have thought many a time since what a wonder it was. The bone of my nose cut right in two, nothing but a bit of skin holding it, and two very large cuts in my head, that two or three pieces of my skull worked out afterwards; and after so long laying on the deck with that very cold weather, and being not altogether drowned, but almost, I think, I did not know I was wounded or loste any blood.

'And now, my dear reader, I am going to show you the hardening nature of sin. When I was struggling in the water for life I gave up all hope, I was dead in my own mind; nevertheless my conscience was so dead asleep I thought nothing about Heaven or hell or judgement; and if I had died then I am sure I should have awaked among devils and damned spirits. See here this great salvation and that of the Lord.'

SMUGGLING ACTIVITIES INCREASE

Virtually every early commentator on the smuggling situation pointed out that as fast as the smugglers were imprisoned or press-ganged into the Navy, others stepped forward into their shoes. In 1733, for example, the Treasury was told in writing by the Commissioners of Customs that immense smuggling was going on in Suffolk, Essex, Kent and Sussex, despite their best efforts to put a stop to it.

In a period of twelve months, to show that the Revenue officers had not been idle, 54,000lb of tea and 123,000 gallons of brandy had been seized, yet smuggling was on the increase. The report says that cargoes were being run by 'well armed gangs', desperate fellows who defied sheriffs and customs officers. In the archives of the customs department there is the following letter, dated 18 May 1733, from the collector of customs at Inverness:

'Yesterday morning some ill-disposed villains have carried away the Customs House boat across the ferry, and with saws and axes have cut her in two by the middle, left the one half on the beach and disposed of the other to the waves.

'The execution of this is owing no doubt to the common people, but the contrivance to greater heads, and that it had been premeditated, appears by the tools they had provided themselves with to perform it.

' 'Tis hard to tell where this will end. The watch house has been twice broken open, the boat destroyed, the expresses from the out ports stopped, and the letters taken away. A person under suspicion of being an informer dragged across the Forth and his ears cut off, and hints given every day to myself to take care of my life; in short, no part of the face of the earth is peopled by such abandoned villains as this country.'

A little later in the history of smuggling in the south there were odd attempts to reach an accommodation with these fearsome smugglers: it was almost as if, not being able to beat them, the authorities tried to get them on their side by connivance! John Banks, the great historian of smuggling in the South East, describes the situation:

'At the commencement of the nineteenth century the Government connived at smuggling, and in this way: – If a smuggler was caught by a man-of-war, and would give information of the state of the French harbours, ships, etc he would be allowed to depart, and, moreover, the captain would give him a written certificate of his having rendered important service to the country, so that, if again caught, he was let go scot free.'

Shipwreck by Joseph Mallord William Turner

153

However, John Banks also noted that many of the old inhabitants of Hastings and other places where smuggling was carried on, could still recall, at the end of the nineteenth century, the heart-aches that followed the capture and punishment of a local smuggling vessel and its crew; he remembered the groups of sorrowing people standing at their doors as the waggons went wending their way along the streets, guarded, as one correspondent put it, 'by the heavily armed Coast-blockade, scowling with a malicious pride on the sorrowing people'. Mr Banks again takes up the story:

THE SMUGGLERS ARM THEMSELVES

'The rough bull-dog sort of fashion in which the Coast-blockade men went about their work, at length roused a spirit of resistance among the smugglers, and they began to go armed, first with bats, stout ashen poles, six or eight feet long, and afterwards with firearms. However wrong this might be, and undoubtedly it was wrong, one cannot wonder, after hearing what the Coast-blockade did in the execution of what they supposed to be their duty, that the smugglers adopted these lawless practices. I do not apologise for the smugglers; it would have been better for them to have followed the example set by some of their leaders, and given up smuggling altogether. In a conversation I had some years ago, with a principal smuggler who resided in Hastings, he said "that when fighting began, he left off smuggling, well knowing that in the end the Government would carry too many bats",meaning thereby that the Government would be too strong for the smugglers. It is but justice here to say, that the Hastings smugglers never went armed; they did the running, while others did the fighting, and once fairly caught, they generally gave in.

'On one occasion, a batsman struck one of his companions in mistake. The blow was given across the chest, and the poor fellow was taken to his home at Icklesham, where he died the next morning. Before he died he was sitting in a chair, and at every respiration the blood issued copiously from his mouth, showing the extent of the injuries he had received internally. I believe the batsmen were paid one pound per night.'

SMUGGLING TAKES ADVANTAGE OF THE SEA TRAFFIC

John Banks is a good historian. He reminds us that until the advent of the railways, the easiest and cheapest mode of transport for goods and passengers was by sea – even a journey from London to Margate or Dover would normally be by ship rather than by road. This meant a lot of traffic, and in the busy Thames estuary and elsewhere it was easy for a boat to change identity, as it were, for the purposes of smuggling:

'In those far-off days,' says Mr Banks, 'all maritime towns received nearly all their heavy goods by sea, in coasting vessels; only a few were sent by carriers' waggons, whose pace was something like a snail's gallop. Hastings had its complement of these vessels, which generally loaded on certain days in the various wharves, on the banks of the Thames ie, those which traded between Hastings and the metropolis.

'This mode of carriage had its advantage – it was cheap. It also had its disadvantage – it was not always sure. Owing to bad weather, it would sometimes happen that Hastings, and other towns as well, would be nearly run out of coals, as all the coals were then sea-borne; and not only that, as the grocers' goods also came almost entirely by sea, Christmas has more than once within my knowledge been painfully close, and no plums in the grocer's shops with which to make the Christmas puddings. Housewives were sometimes in great trouble on such occasions; and the young folks drew long faces at the thought of going without the customary pudding.'

A Change Of Identity

'Among the vessels trading between London and Hastings, was one called *The Farmer's Delight*. The carrying trade in which she had been employed had ceased to pay and she was laid up, ie partially dismantled, and hauled up on the beach out of the way of the tide. After being laid up

DRAGOONS DISPERSING SMUGGLERS.

some time, she was bought by a tradesman whose descendants are now living in Hastings. Sometime afterwards two of her former crew, one of whom is now living in Hastings, and who has corroborated the main points in the following transaction, being on board another coasting vessel in the Thames, saw the old *Farmer's Delight* somewhat altered in form and going leisurely up the Thames, and one of them said to the other, "That looks just like our old craft, only they have altered her stern and made her into a Billy Boy."

'The vessel had formerly been rigged as a sloop, ie with one mast, and her stem and stern were alike. In her altered state she had two masts, similar to what is now called "a dandy rig", and she had the ordinary square stern. Her name had also been altered to The *Nancy of Boston*. 'It appears that she was being towed up the Thames by her crew, the captain being the only person on board the vessel. After she had just passed Gravesend, and had got somewhere off Rosherville, the captain saw a boat put off from the Custom-house. Without more ado he cast off the two-rope, and shouted to the crew of the boat to make off. They did so, and quickly rowed to the Essex side of the river, and decamped. One of them, however, a native of Rye, being afterwards in the neighbourhood of Tower Hill, London, and being in his cups, was boasting of how they got away when coming up the river. He was taken into custody, and sent on board a man-of-war for five years.'

The Captain Is Taken Prisoner

'The Custom-house boat's crew boarded the vessel, and the captain, a stout man, placing himself in the companion-way, haughtily demanded what they wanted on board his vessel. Resistance was, of course, out of the question, and the officers proceeded to search, and the result was, that they discovered a large quantity of tobacco stowed away in the hold, covered over with a quantity of barley. Of course the vessel was seized, and the captain was made prisoner. He was conveyed ashore, and was put into the gaol at Gravesend.

'Now it happened that the gaoler was also keeper of the Town Hall, that is, he had to prepare the Hall for all meetings, and of course to attend all official meetings that were, from time to time, held in the Hall. He was an old man, and during his absence his wife had the care of the gaol. All this was well known to the good people of Gravesend, and of course, to the friends of the prisoner Captain, and they laid a plan for his escape.'

The Captain Escapes

'The gaol-keeper being one day in attendance at the Town Hall, a light cart with a smart trotting-horse was driven to a smith's shoeing place in the neighbourhood of the gaol, and two of the captain's friends began a game of pitch and toss, in a narrow street adjoining the gaol, and by their conversation conveyed intelligence to the imprisoned captain what they were about to do. Going to the outer door of the gaol, they rang the bell, which was answered by the old lady, the gaoler's wife. She was immediately seized, gagged, and tied securely into a chair. The captain was quickly fetched out, and as quickly taken to the cart in waiting. Being a big, fat man, his rescuers did not give him time to get up into the cart in the usual way, but bundled him into the back part of it, the tailboard having been left down for the purpose. He was pretty soon out of the town, and he made his escape.'

Various Altercations

The custom of searching fishing boats by excisemen sometimes led to altercations, even when there was nothing contraband on board. There is a tombstone in All Saints churchyard, at Hastings, recording the death of a fisherman named Swaine, who was shot by an officer named England. Swaine objected to his boat being searched, having given his word that he had nothing, but England insisted; Swaine then wrested England's cutlass from him – whereupon England deliberately drew a pistol and shot the poor man dead on the spot, another of the crew being wounded in the arm by the same bullet. England was tried at Horsham for murder, and sentenced to death, but was afterwards pardoned.

THE OWLERS CHASE THE CUSTOMS OFFICERS INTO RYE.

Exciseman Wearne Takes A Tumble

Smuggling was always attended by the very real risk of death or serious injury, but there were more lighthearted punishments and these were, as often as not, inflicted not on the smugglers, but on the excisemen.

Perhaps the most amusing of these – certainly the best from the far South West – is the story told of an excise officer named Roger Wearne. During a gale, a smuggling vessel was driven onto the rocks, and Wearne, hoping to find evidence of smuggling, commandeered a boat and was rowed to the wreck. The crew, however, had all left her in the night, and had taken the vessel's papers with them, thus destroying all evidence of ownership. Her cargo proved to be fine French porcelain, and Wearne, thinking some of the dishes would be useful and ornamental in his own home, surreptitiously filled his baggy trousers with the chinaware. Weighed down by the cargo he was carrying on his person, the excise officer was a bit slow in descending the ladder to the waiting boat, and one of the boatmen becoming impatient, shouted: 'Look alive, Wearne!' at the same time raising an oar and slapping the other playfully on the seat of his trousers.

With a crash such as might have been made by the proverbial bull in a china shop, and with cries of agony as the shattered bits of smashed crockery cut into his flesh, Wearne came tumbling head-over-heels into the small boat. For years thereafter, Wearne was teased by the smugglers, for wherever he appeared along the coast, he was invariably greeted by: 'Look alive, Wearne!'

Two Smugglers Fall Out With Their Agent

In 1818, there arose a curious case which illustrates not only the ingenuity of the smugglers, but also the shady practices to which the legal fraternity were willing to lend themselves in the cause of such clients. The story is also a rare example of smugglers falling out with each other. Two St Just smugglers named Oats and Permewan had been very successful in running goods on the north coast of Cornwall; their activities extended over a considerable area, and in the course of a few months they were said to have landed no less than six cargoes. The historian Alpheus Verril takes up the story:

'In order to ensure greater secrecy, the smugglers had adopted the method of employing an agent – by name Pridham – to whom they made payment for the goods and whose duty it was to settle their accounts with the French merchants. For some time the arrangement appears to have worked fairly well. At length, however, a report reached the smugglers that the remittances, which were always promptly made on their part, were not being forwarded by their agent. Realising that the latter was no longer to be trusted, the smugglers decided to sever the connection. On this, Pridham announced that he would turn king's evidence against them. A meeting between Permewan and the agent was accordingly arranged with a view, if possible, to buying off the evidence, although the lawyer in charge of the smugglers' defence must have realised as clearly as his clients that there was but slight hope of achieving this.

'It appears, however, that a short time before the meeting was to take place, Permewan suggested that he had doubts as to Pridham's ability to recognize him, seeing that they had only met on two occasions, for a few minutes at a time. They therefore decided to take the risk of dressing up a brother of Permewan's in the latter's clothes, and sending him to Devonshire to the appointed interview. In the meantime, the smuggler brother was at pains on the day on which the meeting took place to be seen walking about the streets of Penzance, where he was spoken to by all and sundry.

'By this means an indisputable alibi was established, which so entirely discredited Pridham's evidence as to render it wholly worthless in a court of law.'

THE SMUGGLERS GO FREE

Ultimately, of course, smuggling could take a very serious turn indeed, and when this happened smugglers and excisemen, and even innocent bystanders were killed. But despite rewards, treachery and hard evidence, juries still occasionally refused to convict. In one such case, in 1768, William Odgers, one of the officers of the excise stationed at Porthleven, Cornwall, was murdered by a party of smugglers for reasons which were never clear. The case was made the subject of an inquiry, and a £100 reward was offered to anyone whose information led to the trial and conviction of the killers.

View over Trevone Bay to Gunver Head on the north Cornish coast

As a result Melchisideck Kinsman of Gwennap, and others unknown, were accused. By this time four of the men implicated had escaped to Guernsey and Morlaix, though later it was said that they had not gone abroad, but were hiding underground in the tin mines. Soon it was reported that £500 had been offered to John Hampton, the principal witness for the Crown against the murderers, to go out of the country and stay away for two years. This Hampton refused, and the authorities then granted him seven shillings a week, as he was afraid to go about on his ordinary work; by 1780 he was receiving ten shillings a week.

Eventually three of the supposed murderers gave themselves up and promised to effect the capture of Kinsman, the fourth, which they succeeded in doing after an affray in which one of them was seriously wounded. All four were tried at the assizes – but contrary to the opinion of the judge, and to the amazement of the whole court, they were found not guilty. It was said at the time that there was no doubt that the jury had been bribed by Kinsman's relatives.

Another story, based though it is on tradition rather than on written evidence, will serve to illustrate further the violence to which the smuggling trade occasionally gave rise.

The Press-Gang Takes Its Man

On a rough piece of moorland forming the western slope of Trencrom Hill, in Cornwall, there were two old granite-built cottages which locally went by the name 'Newcastle'. One of these was run as a beer shop, a noted haunt of the smugglers who had excavated a cave nearby where supplies of contraband goods were regularly stored. At this particular time, the end of the eighteenth century, the beer shop happened to be owned by two brothers, one of whom had joined the army. Finding, however, that life in the army was less interesting (and certainly less rewarding) than smuggling, he deserted and returned home.

It so happened that at about this time the press-gang came into the district, and getting wind of the deserter's whereabouts, a party of soldiery suddenly descended one day on the cottage. The door was opened by the other brother, who on learning the cause of the party's arrival, immediately put up a fight. The press-gang, however, proved too strong for him and in the course of the struggle he was killed. Meantime the deserter brother, unaware of the nature of the fight proceeding below, had made a hole in the roof and succeeded in escaping. On entering the house and finding the bird flown, the press-gang took their departure, and the deserter, though he long continued to live in the neighbourhood, was never troubled with their attentions again. The reason popularly given for this was that having killed one brother, they were debarred from laying hands on the other, since the law did not allow of the taking of two men for one.

An Exciseman Is Punished

John English has a splendid, if rather cruel story of a band of Folkestone smugglers who decided to punish a local exciseman who had tried just a little too hard to catch them:

'I remember hearing a story of an officer, who, having stumbled upon an ambuscade of smugglers, was seized, blindfolded, and had his legs bound. They then announced their intention of throwing him over the cliff, and notwithstanding his entreaties, they dragged him to the edge of the cliff and pushed him gradually over, feet foremost, till his arms and shoulders only remained above. He clung by his fingers to the grass, and thus hanging they left him. He passed an hour in the most intense agony, screaming for help and straining every sinew to maintain his hold. At length he could bear the horror of his position no longer, and was about to drop, but at this moment the bandage slipped partially, and he discovered that he was hanging with his feet only two or three feet from the ground. He ascertained that he had been pushed over a shallow chalkpit, and not, as he imagined, over the cliff. It was certainly a cruel business, and a man of weaker mind would in all probability have died from the fright.

'A somewhat similar story is current of an event which took place on Folkestone Harbour. An obnoxious officer was seized by the smugglers, who carried him to the end of the pier, which then terminated near where the flag staff stands. The poor fellow begged so hard for mercy, and for his life to be spared for the sake of his wife and family, that if there was any real intention to injure him, his persecutors relented, and set him at liberty. His life was spared, but he was always afterwards subjected to jibes and jeers.'

A SMUGGLER IS HONOURED

But how did those smugglers fare who were sentenced to serve His Majesty on board ship? Well, one or two achieved great honour, as Mr English records:

'After the battle of Navarino, a Folkestone smuggler named Black was released from naval service and sent home at the expense of the nation for his gallant conduct in that action. The order for his release is still in existence, and is carefully preserved at Dover.'

Border Raiders

The great reduction of duties in 1823 nearly knocked up smuggling in Scotland, but while it has done so in the Highland districts, the high duties still in force in England has brought the centre of active operations to the Borders. Smugglers from the northern and middle reaches of Scotland have marched almost together to the Border districts, where a fire field is open to their talents in introducing spirits legally made in Scotland, not England. The difference in duty is 8s 6d a gallon. On the line of county between Annan and Berwick, from 6,000–7,000 gallons of whisky are smuggled across the border every week. The whisky that can be brought in Scotland for 5s or 6s per gallon can be retailed over the Border to 10s or 11s. The vendors are all bold and hardy peasants. Each person is loaded with a tin canister fitted to his person holding on average 8–10 gallons and as they travel in parlee of from 8–14 armed with bludgeons the excise officers are afraid to interfere.

Weekly Scotsman, 6 June 1908

Over The Rooftops

One famous Border smuggler was Richard Mendham, a carpenter who rose to opulence tho' ignorant of the arts of reading and writing. Indeed he made so much money that he built in a suburb of Berwick, called Spittal, a row of houses. He inhabited one of these. Another was a public house where his friends were wont to meet and hold secret conference with Mendham by crossing the roofs of the intervening houses and descending by a trap stair which admitted them to the alcove of the dining room in Mendham's mansion. A vault, too, beneath Mendham's stable was accessible via a post which turned and gave admittance to a subterranean place of concealment for contraband. Mendham was eventually tried and executed at Jedburgh.

Weekly Scotsman, 13 June 1908

Coffin Carriers

Tho' often baffled by the smugglers' ingenuity, the excisemen or gaugers as known in Scotland, sometimes had luck on their sides and proved quite as sharp as their opponents. During the afternoon of a bright summer day in 1825 when the scenic beauties of Liddendale were at their best, a mournful cortége draped in sombre trappings, moved slowly over the road leading from Newcastleton to the English border. A few days earlier a well-known smuggler had been drowned while unsuccessfully attempting to emulate young Lochinvar, by fording the Esk river where ford there was none and it was to carry through his interment that his friends were now accompanying the black plumed hearse to the place where the body of the deceased was lying.

All went well for several miles of the journey and the mourners were congratulating themselves on the early termination of their journey, when two arrogant and not over-polite excisemen riding up, commanded the procession to stop. One of them dismounted and in the face of loud protestations pulled out the coffin and prized up the lid. They found within 30 gallons of prime Scots whisky on its way across the Border. The hearse and its driver went straight to Annan jail.

Weekly Scotsman, 13 June 1908

Making Money

Burns' native shire – Ayrshire – attained pre-eminence as a centre of smuggling. People otherwise respectable openly took part in the unlawful traffic, the foundations of many present-day fortunes being laid on the profits acquired during those times.

Kilmarnock Standard, November 1908

Transportation

It appears that in January 1816 William Phillmay and his wife Mary came before the justices. She'd been caught illegally distilling whisky in her house in the remote village of Kyle. Naturally enough she and her husband had objected to seeing the machinery by which their livelihood was earned, carted away. Straightaway the fiery cross was sent round and the clansmen, rallying to the summons, hastily pursued the retreating Excise Officers, overtaking them about 1 mile along the road.

Led by the Amazon Mary, armed with a poker of portentous size, a mob of some 20 strong fell upon the luckless excisemen and inflicted on them a most inhuman beating. Indeed so deadly was the onslaught that the officers were soon compelled to relinquish their capture and flee. The Phillmay's triumph was short-lived: she and her husband were sentenced to transportation for seven years for their share in the fight.

Kilmarnock Standard, November 1908

Bladders Wrecked

On January 12, 1816 while two excisemen were searching for smuggled whisky in the neighbourhood of Cruff, they encountered a band of 28 Irishman carrying between them, 140 gallons of whisky in bladders. The excisemen told the Irishmen to hand over their bladders. Instead, the Irishmen put

them all in a heap, round which they formed in circular array and with bludgeons and pistols ready, dared the officers to come and take the prize. Wisely the excisemen retired with what dignity they could amid the jeers of the smugglers.

Weekly Scotsman, 30 October 1909

Tea Talk

It is hardly possible to make any exact estimate of the quantity of tea and foreign spirits imported and made use of by such as ought to be satisfied with the product of their own country, but it falls within everyone's observation that the use of tea has descended to hundreds, for every one that drank it fifteen years ago. And that foreign spirits are become the entertainment of everyone that cannot come at wine.

Some Consideration of the Present State of Scotland, 1744

When the smugglers' goods are laid of land, all hands are at work for his service; cattle and carriages are ready; every farmhouse, every cottage is open for their reception – giving the least information to the customhouse, is in the opinion of the people, branded with infamy. And if any loose informations shall direct the officers to a search, the county is in Arms and nothing less than a detachment of regular troops can protect the officer in his search or fetch the goods to the customhouse when seized.

Some Consideration of the Present State of Scotland, 1744

On Good Terms

In Newquay the smugglers and excisemen were stated to be on excellent terms. It was not uncommon... for a hundred horses to be awaiting the arrival of cargo here every day of the week.

A.K. Hamilton Jenkin *Cornish Seafarers*, 1932

THE CAUTIOUS TURNED THEIR FACES AWAY WHILE THE FREE-TRADERS PASSED."

CONTRABAND

Notorious Character

There was a character notorious on the coast of Northumberland – Scotland right up to Edinburgh – Yawkins, a Dutch skipper. His mere name was a terror to officers of the Revenue. He availed himself of the fears which his presence inspired on one occasion when, happening to be ashore with a considerable amount of goods in his sole custody on which no duty had been paid, a strong party of Excisemen bore down upon him. Instead of bolting in the face of superior force he sprang among them, shouting: 'Yawkins is before you! Come on my lads?' The Revenue men were so surprised they fled.

Once, when landing his cargo near Kirkcudbright, two Revenue cutters, the *Pigmy* and the *Dwarf* simultaneously hove in sight... on different tacks, the one coming round by the isles of Fleet the other between the Point of Rueberry and the Muckle Ron. The dauntless free trader instantly weighed anchor and bore down right between the luggers, so close that he tossed his hat on the deck of the one and his wig on that of the other, hoisted a cask to his maintop to show his occupation and bore away under an extraordinary pressure of sail without receiving injury. To account for this and other hair-breadth escapes, popular tradition alleged that Yawkins insured himself against capture by a bargain with the evil one. The vessel, famous for many a day, was the *Black Prince*. She visited to discharge her cargo at Luce, Bekarry and elsewhere along the coast, sometimes running as far down as the Tyne and Tees.'

Athol Forbes *The Romance of Smuggling*, 1909

Every Drop

For many years in the early part of the 19th century virtually every drop of whisky and wine drunk in Glasgow had been smuggled in.

Athol Forbes *The Romance of Smuggling*, 1909

Suspect Fruit

A trading vessel put into Leith harbour in December 1821 with a full cargo of apples from Hamburg. Everything seemed fair and square, yet the excisemen insisted on prying into the sweet-smelling contents of the casks. There they found a very large amount of foreign silk, neatly done up in parcels, rolled in lead sheet and snugly stowed in the midst of the luscious fruit. The lead taking the impress of the great weight of apples both above and below it, retained its position immovably and being at the same time, absolutely waterproof, preserved the smuggle as no other wrapping would. On another occasion a casting vessel from the north put in at Leith with hundreds of geese ready plucked aboard. Each contained a bottle of whisky!

Athol Forbes *The Romance of Smuggling*, 1909

Cork Jacket

An old seaman used to tell a story that an old gipsy woman had told him that one day he would be drowned. He used to tell everyone this story to explain why he always wore a cork jacket, which he was fond of exhibiting. When the Customs House officers came aboard he would insist on going through the whole story and the performance of showing the cork jacket.

They knew the yarn by heart and were glad to escape from him, but the wily old sea dog has retired on a comfortable little property, and small amounts of tobacco secreted in that celebrated cork jacket – and successfully landed – have combined to make up a nice bank balance. The life-saving appliance was also a money-saving one. The old seaman winks one eye when pressed on the gipsy's phrophecy(?): 'Wonderful people, them gipsies – saved my life and more.'

Athol Forbes *The Romance of Smuggling*, 1909

Enough To Convert Any Man

'Yes, sir, he was very much respected; and you'll not be surprised after what I told you before. He stuck to his trade as long as he was able to go afloat; and when he got too old for that he took to lighter jobs – some on 'em take to drink, but old dad being an educated man cottoned on to his Bible, which was werry right and proper at his time of life. Yes, sir, every Sunday afternoon, as soon as dinner was stowed and he'd had his pipe, mother'd bring out the family Bible and before you could say knife the old chap had settled his head onto it and would be snoring away like a steam hooter in fog.

'Maybe you'll have heard how the old man did a bit of free-trading in his day – smuggling they calls it now! Well, before he coiled his ropes up for a full due, he used to go on a deal about that there free-trade, saying on it was a wrong thing to do. Cos why? Cos there weren't no sartinty about it. You never knew where you were – come today, gone tomorrow! Will, sure enough twas a falterin sort of business. I don't wonder the old man see'd the wickedness of it after losing that last crop of goods down by Hemmick Cove, yonder. Aye, 'twas enough to convert any man!'

H.N. Shore *Old Foye Days*, 1909

THE CUSTOM HOUSE, LONDON, IN THE REIGN OF QUEEN ELIZABETH

Prominent Women

Dover town was about this time [in the 1820s] the scene of stirring events. One Lieutenant Lilburn, in command of a revenue cutter, had captured a smuggler and placed the crew in Dover jail. They were not faced with the death penalty as they had not offered armed resistance, but they were liable to service aboard a man 'o war – a fate they were most anxious to avoid. These imprisoned men were largely natives of Folkestone and Sandgate and their relatives determined to march the ten miles between these places and Dover and, if possible, literate them. When they arrived in Dover and their intention became known, a crowd of fisherfolk and longshore people swarmed out of the Dover alleyways and reinforced them.

Prominent among them were the women, who as ever in cases of popular tumult, proved themselves the most violent and destructive among the mob. Nothing less than the destruction of the gaol was decided upon, and the more active spirits climbed upon the roof and from that vantage point showered bricks and tiles upon the mayor and soldiers who had been called out. The mayor, beset with tooth and claw by angry women – who tore the riot act out of his hand – fled, and Lieut. Lilburn exhorted the officer in charge of the military to fire upon the crowd, but he declined. Meanwhile the tradespeople busied themselves barricading their shops. The prisoners were triumphantly liberated.

Charles Harper *The Smugglers*, 1909

Tobacco To Ireland

American vessels were in the habit of depositing cargoes of tobacco on the north shores of Ireland, great numbers of the peasantry volunteering assistance at the running. From thence the contraband was borne by various craft to the coast of Ayrshire whence carriers conveyed it to Glasgow in bundles of 60–100lb.

W. Thomson *The Smuggling Era in Scotland*, 1910

The Smuggler Captain's Song

'Fire on, fire on,' says Captain Ward
'I value you not a pin;
If you are brass on the outside,
I am steel within.

'Go home, go home,' says Captain Ward
'And tell your King from me,
If he reigns King upon dry land
I will reign at sea.'

Old song (Quoted in *Traditions and Hearthside Stories of West Cornwall* by William Bottrell, 1870)

Confined to Bed

Smuggling in Mousehole had arrived at such a pitch towards the end of the 18th century that the goods were commonly carried at midday, the local excise-man excusing himself on one of these occasions by stating that he was confined to his bed through having been pelted with stones a few days earlier.

A.K. Hamilton Jenkin *Cornish Seafarers*, 1932

A Bladder Of Spirits

On Thursday, January 11, 1816 between 7pm–8pm, two customs officials intercepted at Townhead Toll four burly ruffians safeguarding the transit of a single bladder of spirits. This they not only refused to give up, but the bearer, with heavy bludgeon raised, rushed on one of the excisemen and fiercely assailed him. The latter being very strong, seized his opponent and managed to drag him to the Bell o' the Brae, while the other gauger with drawn cutlass, kept at bay the other smugglers, though the rapidly gathering and none too friendly crowd greatly impeded their movements. Repeatedly the leading smuggler grasped the blade of the officer's cutlass and the efforts to release this weapon, his hands became horribly gashed. By and by a police patrol came tardily on the scene and with their help the prisoner was conveyed to a point opposite the gales of the old college. Here his friends closed up to support him and made an onslaught so irresistible that in the end the constables fled for their lives and the smugglers got clear away. Next morning the excisemen learned, to their chagrin, that all this uproar and commotion, all the direful din and confusion at the Bell o' the Brae, had been raised as a blind to cover the safe running of a huge load of contraband elsewhere.

Weekly Scotsman, 9 October 1909

Price Of Whisky

In the early 19th century, Glasgow distillers admitted the illegally distilled whisky was better than theirs. At this time illegal whisky cost four shillings a gallon – legal whisky cost nine shillings and six pence. Among illicit distillers in Glasgow a favourable dodge was to erect their apparatus in the house of some person so wretchedly poor that the justices, commiserating their condition, greatly reduced or altogether dispensed with the fines.

A glowing case in point came under notice in December 1821 when a woman actually on the poor roll was convicted and penalised for having a large illicit still in her house. She declared it belonged to several of her male lodgers of whose movements she was unaware. She was fined £20, afterwards modified to £5. The real culprits paid the £5.

W. Thomson *The Smuggling Era in Scotland*, 1910

A Mother's Means

In July 1822 a young man, unable to pay the fine inflicted for his breaches of customs and excise law, was incarcerated in Glasgow Gaol, till such times as he could.

Thither on the first evening of his detention went his mother and sister to coddle and sympathise with their loved one. After a little while spent in each other's company, mother and daughter passed through the prison gates weeping bitterly, the former begging the gaoler to be kind to her only laddie. This he promised would be done, but imagine his surprise when on visiting the smuggler's cell soon after, he found in the sole occupant a buxom young woman whose brother, disguised in spare clothing brought by his relatives and with tartan plaid drawn closely over his head, had safely passed the prison gates under the very nose of the guardian thereof. Nor was this the end of the matter, for the crown authorities becoming aware of the prisoner's escape sued the Magistrate of Glasgow for payment of his fine and this, to the amount of £29 18s, they were compelled to pay.

W. Thomson *The Smuggling Era in Scotland*, 1910

The Smuggling Mayor

Much of the reckless daring of the smugglers at this time was undoubtedly due to the fact that they enjoyed the protection of, and not infrequently an actual alliance with, local officials. In 1770, the Mayor of Penzance was actually bound over in a considerable sum 'not to be again guilty of smuggling'. In 1794, four persons belonging to Poughill and Madron were prosecuted for having evaded the customs on smuggled goods to the extent of £18,600. They offered £160 in compensation. One was a small farmer, whose property was worth just £15 a year; another a labourer, working for him. The two others were small yeomen.

T.V. Holmes, 'Transactions of the Cumberland & Westmoreland Assocn,' 1891

Scottish Prices

Whisky, however, remained in its old position in spite of a desperate affray which took place on Eden Bridge in 1824 between smugglers and excisemen, followed a few days after by one hundred and twenty informations against publicans for selling smuggled spirits; a fact which testifies in the most unquestionable way to the immense demand in Carlisle for whisky at

Scottish prices. Yet more than a quarter of a century was to elapse before the equalisation of the excise duty on spirits on both sides of the Border, an event which happened in 1852 or 1853.

T.V. Holmes, 'Transactions of the Cumberland & Westmorland Assocn', 1891

Enter A Bond

Aproclamation issued in 1805 said any smuggler who'd escaped abroad could return provided he entered into a bond to smuggle no more.

A.K. Hamilton Jenkin *Cornish Seafarers*, 1932

Plaster Of Paris

Formerly vessels freighted with chalk frequently unloaded at Hastings, and on one occasion a free trader, in order to deceive the blockade, had a cargo of tubs coated over with plaster of Paris, roughly put on. It happened that when the cargo was being unloaded, as if it were chalk, one of these manufactured lumps slipped off the cart while it was going up the beach. A Coast-blockade man coming along, began to poke it about with the point of his cutlass, which after a little, stuck in the cask, and let out the brandy and the secret.

John Banks *Reminiscences of Old Folkestone Smugglers*, 1873

The Smuggler King

There's a brave little bark stealing out in the dark,
From her nest in the bristling bay;
The fresh breeze meets her dingy sheets,
    And swiftly she darts away;
She never must run in the eyes of the sun,
    But along with the owl take wing,
She must keep her flight for the moonlight night,
    For she carries the Smuggler King.
A monarch is he as proud as can be
    Of a strong and mighty band,
The bullet and blast may go whistling past,
    But he quails neither heart nor hand.
He lives and dies with his fearful prize
Like a hunted wolf he'll spring,
With trigger and dirk, to the deadliest work,
And fight like a Smuggler King.
Back from the wave, to his home in the cave,
In the sheen of the torches' glare;
He reigns the lord of a freebooter's board,
    And never was costlier fare.
Right firm and true were the hearts of the crew,
There's faith in the shouts that ring
As they stave the cask, and drain the flask,
And drink to the Smuggler King.

Smuggling In Poole

'Sir, Damn thee
and God Damn thy two Purblind Eyes thou Buger and thou Death looking Son of a Bitch O that I had bin there (with my company) for they sake when thou tookes them men of Mine on Board the Speedwell Cutter on Monday ye 14 Decr. I would drove thee and all they Gang to Hell wher thou belongest thou Devil Incarnet Go Down thou Hell Hound into thy Kennell below & Bathe thy Self in that Sulpherous Lake that has bin so long Prepared for such as thee for it is time the World was rid of such a Monster thou art no Man but a Devil thou fiend I hope thou will soon fall into Hell like a star from the Sky; there to lie (unpitied) & unrelented of any for Ever and Ever Which God Grant of his Infinite Mercy Amen'

Letter from J. Spurier, smuggler;
Fordingbridge, January 1700

GHOSTS & GHOULS

The secretive nature of smuggling makes it a rich source of scary stories – these might be of mysterious disappearances, of phantoms seen by the light of the moon, or simply of inexplicable noises heard in lonely old houses. Often, of course, stories of ghosts and ghouls were simply invented by the smugglers to frighten off the over-inquisitive from houses and pubs where contraband was stored, but something invented initially for effect soon took on a life of its own as it was told and re-told down the generations. When it came to inventing ghosts the smugglers didn't have it all their own way, however, as the following story from Yorkshire reveals. It comes from a number of sources.

Smugglers were always superstitious, and believed that the phantoms of their drowned or hanged comrades would always haunt the river, the beach and the cliffs. It was held to be unlucky for one smuggler to see the ghost of another, and even more unlucky to have one speak to you. Sailors disliked walking at night near the rocks or beach that had been the scene of a shipwreck, as they are supposed to be visited by the ghosts of the men who manned the doomed vessels. Frequently a fisherman would declare that he had heard the voices of his dead mates hailing him.

A GHOSTLY RUSE

One moonlit night in the 1860s a coastguardsman by the name of Murray was doing his patrol from Hartlepool to Black Hall Rocks when his attention was attracted to a small boat making for the shore in the vicinity of Crimdon Dene. With his companion, coast-guardsman Hicks, Murray walked down from the sandhills and hailed the men in the boat. He straightaway recognised one as a notorious smuggler, and guessed what his purpose was. But to attempt the arrest of seven or eight men meant danger, and would almost certainly fail.

Murray was ingenious, however. He retreated and made his way to a cottage, where he borrowed a white sheet. Hicks continued on the beat, but Murray, taking advantage of the shelter afforded by some rocks to the north of the Dene, waded into the sea and worked his way to the scene of operations. The men were expeditiously transferring the contraband from the boat to the shore, keeping a sharp look-out from time to time along the coast. Suddenly the man in the boat gave a shriek, leaped out into the water and ran as best he could for the beach. He was speechless with terror: three of his companions endeavoured to obtain an explanation, but in vain, so came back to the boat. Then a melancholy voice wailed from the water, 'Matthew Horsley! Matthew Horsley!' And in the dim distance the men saw a white ghostly figure rising out of the water and moving towards them.

The spell of the moon upon the dripping sheet which enveloped Murray, the voice, and the solemn murmur of the waves, all combined to produce a feeling calculated to test the nerves of most ordinary beings – to men who believed in such apparitions as surely as they believed in their own existence, the effect was utterly demoralising. With frenzied yells they rushed for the shore, and the coastguardsman was left in undisturbed possession of the smuggled goods. He carefully marked everything with the broad arrow

stamp, the government sign of possession, and waited for his mate who had to meet him on that beat.

But coastguardsmen themselves were not free from this kind of superstition, and as coastguardsman Hicks came upon the scene described above, his first sight of it was a spectral figure in the boat glistening in the moonlight. He satisfied himself that it was a real figure, and started off to make his report at headquarters without further investigation – and when the figure called him by name, he put on an extra spurt.

The following day Murray was complimented by his chief and received a substantial recognition for a very smart capture of three hundredweight of tobacco, and of course the boat.

Similar tales have come down to us from pretty much every coastal area where smuggling was once prevalent, but one of the best – though it is only tenuously connected with smuggling – is the tale or mystery of Kitty Cannom, a story from the misty marshes of Essex. It is gleaned largely from *The Cambridge Journal* which published the story originally in August 1752:

THE OWLERS.

THE MYSTERY OF THE EMBALMED LADY

'One squally day early in July 1752, a small coasting vessel beat up the estuary of the Colne, and dropped anchor a short distance below Colchester. Ever on the alert, some Revenue officers noticed that several chests were being landed ashore, and promptly proceeded to investigate. A polite young man of about twenty-five years of age, who, speaking in French, gave his name as Mr Williams and his calling as that of a Hamburg merchant, declared these chests to be his property. They were duly overhauled – all except one – and found to contain much jewellery and costly feminine wearing apparel. The remaining chest, a case of large size, Mr Williams endeavoured to retain intact, declaring that its contents must not be examined. Suspicion at once deepened on the part of the Revenue men, both as regards the questionable coffer and its owner. Mr Williams protested volubly; he raved, he asserted that the chest contained the body of his dear, dear wife, and even produced what purported to be a letter from the King of France in support of his *bona fides*; but all to no purpose.

The usual rough-and-ready method of procedure in such cases was to run an instrument through the package and then test for the nature of its contents. One of the Customs men, who had more respect for his duty than for the King of France, had actually drawn his sword for the purpose mentioned, when instantly the quasi-Hamburg merchant (who wore a sword) intimated that if any running through had to take place, it would in fact be effected on the body of the person who attempted to commit such an outrage.

And yet the Revenue men were not dismayed, for while Mr Williams was forcibly restrained, the unpacking proceeded with methodical precision. And all the time Mr Williams, like the heathen, raged furiously. At length the last of the wrappings was unwound, when behold, the embalmed body of a beautiful woman was disclosed to view.

Here was a pretty situation. Nothing daunted, and still suspecting some trick, or worse still, a horrible crime, the authorities had the cadaver removed to the Parish Church at Hythe, where it was set up in the vestry for purposes of identification. Not a few curious people availed themselves of the opportunity of gazing at such a spectacle, and all the time Mr Williams continued to lament – which is scarcely to be wondered at. Methods in those days were not of the kid-glove variety, and little respect was shown to delicate susceptibilities. A further mystery was sensed, and those in authority were determined not to be hoodwinked. The corpse was refused burial, although Mr Williams, who was detained in the church (failing a more convenient prison), was allowed access to the vestry where he apparently passed several days and nights in company with the dead woman.

In Georgian days it was somewhat difficult to procure interment for a deceased person on whom an embargo had been placed. As some analogy to the drastic and insalubrious measures just related, it will be remembered that as late as 1816, sixty-four years after the events we are now dealing with, the corpse of Richard Brinsley Sheridan was formally arrested by a bailiff, who successfully prevented the removal of the remains for burial until a debt of £500 incurred by the great orator had been settled.

The smugglers tell their tales: Teignmouth by Moonlight *by Thomas Luny*

No one knows how the Essex mystery would have ended if, amongst the visitors to Hythe Church, there had not arrived a certain benevolent gentleman who spoke French fluently, and showed an interest in the unhappy young man incarcerated there. His sympathy evoked a burst of confidence from the prisoner, who imparted to the stranger a narration which reads more like a romance from the pen of Cervantes or Le Sage than a prosaic description of an English domestic tragedy.

His name, it transpired, was not Williams, neither was his condition that of a Hamburg merchant. Indeed, he was a *person of quality*, and some of these early printed accounts reported him as being Lord Delamere, son of the Earl of Rosebery – a conjunction of titles that does not seem to dovetail. (Later on, when evidence began to crystallize, the appellation of Delamere was corrected to that of Dalmeny.) His version of the matter was as follows: he was born in Florence, and had never visited England till some three years previously, when in London he first met the deceased lady, who appears to have been some five or six years his senior, and fell desperately in love with her. They were married, and during the intervening period had travelled much abroad. Failure of the lady's health culminated in a rapid decline, but before she died she left a brief written confession that her maiden name was Catherine Cannom (Canham) and that she was actually the wife of the Rev

Alexander Gough, rector (vicar) of Thorpe-le-Soken in Essex; her last wish was that her body might be buried in that parish.

My lord was shocked at the disclosure, but endeavoured to carry out the lady's dying wishes, and would have done so but for the interference of the customs officers. The body was embalmed at Verona, and after traversing France, it was placed on board a ship bound for Dover. On arrival, another vessel was chartered to take it to Harwich, but owing to the roughness of the weather the second ship was driven farther down the coast so that embarkation had to be effected elsewhere. My lord protested that he had been entirely ignorant of any previous marriage, and in floods of tears he expressed his desire to be buried in the same grave with his lady.

The foregoing statement may be taken as verbally correct, since it was communicated to the press by the brother of the sympathetic gentleman, who was probably some local personage. It is even said that when he was allowed a sight of the deceased lady's face the gentleman at once recognised the features as those of Mrs Gough, née Kitty Cannom.

The Rev Alexander Gough was at once communicated with, but he was transported with fury and proceeded to behave in a most unclerical manner, threatening to run his wife's last husband through the body. (It may be observed that there is a good deal of this sort of menace throughout the narrative.) Anyhow, the reverend gentleman and his successor to the deceased lady's affections eventually made matters up, and since by this time the suspicions of the Customs authorities were allayed, the corpse was placed in a sumptuous coffin and transported to Thorpe-le-Soken, where both "husbands" attended the funeral in deep mourning.

There are some unimportant discrepancies in this tale, but taking it as an example of eighteenth-century procedure and manners, the whole affair, while being a trifle grisly, is decidedly enlightening. Moreover it is quite possible that an embalmed corpse transported from abroad and to be taken to the Soken district did not diminish the shrewd concern of the Customs, because the region was notoriously a great centre for smuggling operations, and difficult to supervise. A cave still exists in the vicinity of Landermere, near Thorpe, which tradition points out as once being a 'hide' for contraband goods, and mock funerals were not unknown to the Preventive force – though in this particular case their zeal evidently led them to a wrong conclusion.

THE DANISH IMPOSTER

We move further into the world of Gothic horror with the next story, which has a number of sources, both oral and written. Few would accept it literally today, but it shows the extent to which the smuggler had infiltrated the very myths of a county noted for a scarcely concealed belief in spirits and the underworld. Certainly no eighteenth-century Cornish smuggler earned greater notoriety than Cruel Coppinger, the Dane, and a number of authors – including the Rev R. S. Hawker (in his book *Former Men in Far Cornwall*) and William Bottrell (in his *Traditions and Hearthside Stories of West Cornwall*) – have recounted the following tale:

Local tradition relates that one day in the midst of a fearful storm a foreign-rigged vessel was seen drifting in towards the shore. Whether or not she was actually wrecked was never known, for the ship was soon afterwards lost to sight in the driving clouds and rain. One man, however, came ashore from her, swimming powerfully through the boiling surf. Wrapped in a cloak that he is said to have torn from the shoulders of an old woman who was on the beach, the stranger leaped up behind a farmer's daughter who had ridden down to see the wreck, and was taken by her to her father's house, where he was fed, clothed, and most hospitably received.

He was a fine, handsome, well built man, and claimed to be highly connected in his own country. He soon won the young woman's affections, and at her father's death, which occurred not long after, he easily induced her to marry him. The union was not a happy one, however, and – fortunately perhaps – there was only one child, a deaf and dumb idiot who inherited his father's cruel disposition; he delighted in torturing all living things, and it is even said that he cunningly killed one of his young playmates.

After his marriage, Coppinger made himself the captain of an organised band of smugglers, and through his black deeds quickly earned the title by which he is remembered. Hawker in his book refers to Coppinger's ship as the *Black Prince*, and informs us that he had it built for himself in Denmark; he also reports that men who had made themselves in any way obnoxious to him on land were carried on board this vessel and compelled, by fearful oaths, to enrol themselves as members of her crew. And although Hawker was a novelist rather than an historian, there is no reason for doubting this particular assertion. In the year 1835, an old man of the age of ninety-seven, told Miss M. A. Courtney, of Penzance, that when he was a youth he had been abducted in a precisely similar manner, and had only been ransomed by his friends after two years' service on board a smuggling craft.

An owler's lantern used on the Essex marshes. It was designed so that the light only shone from the front making it visible only to the smugglers' boat waiting at sea

'And all because I happened to see one man kill another, and they thought that I should mention it,' said the old man, very simply.

The Dane's Deathbed

Hawker, who delighted in flights of the imagination, whether his own or those of the simple country folk among whom he lived, credits Coppinger with a wondrous and fearful end. His account, however, tallies closely with that given by many others of the passing of a wicked and notorious wrecker near St Just; the tale goes as follows:

At length the time came for the Devil to claim his own. Several parsons and other pious folk were sent for and readily came, because the dying sinner was rich. Although it was harvest time and mid-day, the old wrecker's chamber became, at times, as dark as night. The parsons saw the Devil in the room when others could not, and by their Bible reading they drove him to take many shapes – but for all that he would not be put out, and at last, when he took the form of a fly and buzzed about the dying wretch, they saw that it was useless for them to try any longer.

During all the time the exorcists were thus engaged, the chamber seemed – by the sound – to be filled with the sea splashing around the bed, and waves were heard as if surging and breaking against the house, though it was a good bit inland.

The Ship Of Doom

While this was taking place at the dying man's bedside, two men, who were busy with harvest work in one of his fields near the cliff, heard a hollow voice, as if coming from the sea, which said, 'The hour is come, but the man is not come.' Looking in the direction from whence the words proceeded, they saw no person; but far out to sea they beheld a black, heavy, square-rigged ship, with all sail set, coming in fast, against wind and tide and not a hand to be seen aboard her. She came so close under the cliff that only her topmast could be seen; and then black clouds, that seemed to rise out of the deep, gathered around her, and extended straight to the dying man's chamber. The harvesters, terrified at the sight of this ship of doom so near them, ran up to the town-place – and just at this moment the old sinner died, and his dwelling shook as if about to fall.

Everybody, in a great fright, rushed out and saw the black clouds roll off towards the death-ship, which at once sailed away amidst a blaze of lightning over the sea, and disappeared. The weather immediately cleared, and nothing unusual occurred until a few men assembled to put the wrecker's ghastly remains quickly off the face of the earth. Then, as the coffin was borne towards the churchyard, the sky again became suddenly overcast, and a tempest sprang up with such violence that they could scarcely keep on their legs to reach the churchyard stile, where such sheets of blinding lightning flashed around them that they dropped the coffin and rushed into the church. The storm having at length abated, they ventured out to find nothing of the coffin but its handles and a few nails, all else having been set on fire and consumed by the lightning. And that was the end of Cruel Coppinger.

Coppinger must have been a terrifying individual for such an extraordinary story to have been told of him – but then storytelling has always been a feature of the smuggler's world, perhaps the result of those long waits on lonely beaches and headlands.

HAUNTED HOUSES

Telling the tale of Coppinger would not be to the advantage of any smuggler, but tales of ghosts and ghouls were often invented in order to scare the excisemen off. The smugglers often let it be known, for example, that a lonely house on the cliff or the marshes was

Tales of smugglers' derring-do are rich fodder for young, impressionable minds

haunted; or they said that a man in a certain cottage was ill with the smallpox, or that a certain inn was bewitched, and naturally everyone would avoid it, giving the smugglers plenty of chance to stow their cargo without interruption.

Houses and pubs with hidden rooms, cellars and secret passageways were bound to generate spooky stories. But the most extraordinary piece of tunnel building, with its own ghostly tale, must be that discovered at Margate in Kent. The story, and an account of similar earthworks, is told in Banks's *Reminiscences of Old Folkestone Smugglers*:

'In 1832 a tunnel was discovered by the coastguards cut through the chalk cliff at Margate for a distance of 200 yards from the sea shore to a house in the town. At the beginning of the century I am informed that a somewhat similar discovery was made in a house near Folkestone, standing not far from the sea. It was let to a tenant apparently of good social standing, but at the end of six months or thereabouts he gave out that it was haunted. The owner disbelieved this statement, and went to reside in it himself, in order to unravel the mystery, if possible. He was unsuccessful, however, and as his dreams were nightly disturbed by horrid noises, he at length retired from the place, baffled.

'The house stood empty for a long time, the grounds became over-run with rank vegetation, and the place altogether presented a ruinous and desolate appearance. The solution of the mystery was at length discovered by accident. A romantic young fellow was determined to get at the bottom of the matter, and night after night he prowled round and round the place, anxiously seeking for some clue, until one night, after many weary nights of watching, he perceived a light shining through the closed shutters in the basement. The key was kept by an innkeeper nearby, and having obtained it, the explorer went again the next night, and made his way to the cellars, where he found a large quantity of contraband goods comfortably stowed away. Further investigation showed that there was access from the cellar to the shore, and by this means the goods had been conveyed to the haunted house. Fortunately for the smugglers, they were none of them on the premises when the discovery was made, and the tenant who proclaimed the house to be haunted never again showed his face in this locality.'

A Reputed Sorceress

The Celts have always been partial to stories of things that go bump in the night, but tradition north of the Border often implicates women in the ghostly activities, as the following tale from the *Kilmarnock Standard* for November 1908 reveals:

'On the coast of Carrick [in Ayrshire] mischievous spirits were supposed to guard the places where contraband was concealed and were even known to attack too adventurous excisemen. Aged women received and concealed stores and passed, by repute, for witches. Coffins carried on the back of demons were often seen during the night near these women's houses. About a century ago Kate Steen, a reputed sorceress, flourished at Kirk Uswald. She was so popular among the tenant farmers that she was sustained by their gifts. In her one-room house was a deep hold in which the contents of many a smuggling lugger found a temporary home. Over its entrance, covered with grass and rushes, she sat at her spinning wheel, the picture of aged innocence and simplicity.'

OVER THE BORDER

Smuggling in Scotland was always rather different in some respects from smuggling in other parts of Britain. Certainly a great deal of contraband came into the country in the usual way — that is, by sea from France, Holland and elsewhere – but the bulk of Scottish smuggling was over the border into England. The reason for this, as readers will already have gathered, was that the tax payable on English whisky was much higher than that paid on Scottish. This meant there was a great deal of money to be earned by anyone enterprising enough to shift the stuff over the border. Better still, almost everyone in Scotland, but particularly in the highlands, had access, for free, to everything necessary to make their own whisky. The situation must have seemed heaven sent – except to the excisemen who were bedevilled by the remoteness of the countryside and the superior knowledge of tracks and trails of the smugglers.

THE SMUGGLERS' HORSES

The Scots were brilliantly inventive smugglers, but if the following story is to be believed, their horses were remarkably intelligent, too. It comes from the *Dumfries and Galloway Magazine*:

'The aid which smugglers frequently derived from a troop of well trained horses is too well known to many of the old inhabitants of Dumfries and the surrounding country to require much illustration here. Several individuals are yet alive, or at least were very lately, who can remember the astonishing performances of one of these troops in particular. The writer has frequently been told that it was no unusual circumstance at an early hour of the morning to see this band heavily laden with contraband goods unattended by any human being, and preceded by a white horse of surprising sagacity, scouring along the Old Bridge down the White Sands and through the streets of Dumfries without any one daring to interrupt their progress.

'Indeed, in those days such an attempt was not likely to be often made, for it is notorious that the inhabitants themselves were too deeply implicated in similar transactions to induce them to restrain others. It is related however, that on one or two occasions, when some individual more officious than the rest rashly attempted to intercept the leader of the

An illustration from the Illustrated London News *shows horses standing ready to carry yet another consignment of contraband*

troop, the wily animal either suddenly reared and struck its opposer to the ground, or by a peculiar motion swung the kegs, with which it was almost always loaded, with so much violence that no one durst approach within its reach.'

THE TOLL KEEPER OF GRETNA

The craft of human smuggling was no less impressive, and it produced stories that now enjoy legendary status. A case in point is the story of the crafty toll keeper of Gretna. Again the story comes from the *Dumfries and Galloway Magazine*:

'Having been checked by legislation, another system of smuggling sprang up, viz, the carrying of the whisky across the Border in skins and tin casks, which has also now ceased, owing to the alteration of revenue laws, by a wise equalisation of the duty in Scotland with that of England. Large casks of whisky were brought from Leith by carriers to supply the spirit merchants of Annan. Several puncheons would often be disposed of in a night to gangs who proceeded across the Firth, the difference of duty (4s or 5s gallon) being the gain for the risk of detection by the revenue officers.

'In connection with this Border smuggling, there is a story told of one of its devotees. On his way across the Border with several kegs in the bottom of his light cart, he was obliged to stop at a toll-bar somewhere near Gretna to awaken the keeper to let him through. While hailing this functionary, an exciseman pounced upon him from behind the house and arrested cart, kegs, smuggler and all. The horse's head was turned Annanwards, the Customs officer, quite proud of himself, walking with the smuggler at the horse's head. But the toll-keeper grasping the whole situation, quietly slipped after them, and aided by the darkness as the cart rumbled on, he noiselessly removed a keg and laid it quietly down at the roadside. A second time, and even a third time he repeated this, the exciseman and his prisoner little thinking of what was happening behind them.

'On reaching Annan, a triumphant report was made to his superiors by the exciseman, and his mortification can well be imagined when the cart was examined and found empty. One rather wonders what the smuggler thought of it all.'

A Smuggler Is Shot

'In the year 1822 a man named Harding, of Great Corby, was shot by an exciseman named Forster, while endeavouring to smuggle three stones of salt in order to cure his pig, an incident which may have had some influence in causing the great reduction of salt duty in 1823.'

In his turn-of-the-century book *The Smuggling Era in Scotland*, William Thomson remembered Blether Jock, the sort of remarkable character that a country teeming with smugglers and smuggling stories was bound to produce:

The Well-To-Do Pedlar

'When I was a very small boy, an old man living in a snug little wood-begirt cottage near Lochenbreck Spa, told me a story of his youth, associated with the remnant of smugglers of whisky, brandy and tobacco. In a smaller way than was the custom of the earlier smugglers, they disposed of illicit cargoes among the hills of Galloway and Ayrshire, in what might be called a retail way.

'Blether Jock was looked upon by everyone who knew him, not as a gangrel or half-witted beggar, but rather as a well-to-do pedlar, with a curious eccentricity of unwillingness to show his pack of goods. He made periodical visits over his own particular route among the wilder parts of the country, and was rarely observed moving about during the day, but usually "daunert in aboot the gloamin".

'He was in the habit of carrying on his back and upon his person what he termed his "ain bedding", which looked like a huge pack. This, Jock was always careful to keep under his keen eye at all times when unburdened of his load. A large, round bundle, it was wrapped in a blue home-made blanket. The contents of this pack was nothing less than a basket made from dried rushes, constructed somewhat on the plan of a wasps' nest. Each cell contained a bladder of whisky or brandy. The inside of his long shaggy coat was also a

Many a Highland cottage heard the midnight knock at the door

stowing-place for tobacco, or any small pieces of stuff he could pick up from the curious ports where he got his wholesale supplies.

'Jock would call at one of the moor houses, usually shepherds' cottages, and in due time be snugly stowed in the byre or barn for the night. The shepherd would say nothing till Jock was supposed to be asleep, when he would make an errand to the byre to see that all the cattle were right before he would retire. This was to get his two or three bladders of whisky, etc, from Jock and to pay for the same. Next day Jock would wander over the hills to another customer, and thus dispose of his cargo, his blanket pack never to appearance altering in bulk, if lighter in weight. Jock, the old man told me, was one of a numerous gang who plied this kind of trade all over Scotland, and did so successfully for many years after the Solway was supposed to be cleared of the smugglers.

'The old man added: "Ay, mun, monies the blethers my faither got frae Jock awa' owerby there aboot Culcaigrie," and added that, "there was anither gang that a hae' got whusky frae, but they had nocht at a' adae with' the sea-smugglers; they cam' awa' frae the Heelins wi't, juist like Jock in blethers, but the stuff was coorse raw Heilan' whusky, made in sma' stells throughout the Heelins, and twa gills o't wud hae filled ye as fou as a piper.'

A Cat-And-Mouse Game

In the north of Scotland and on the Western Isles there was a similar tradition of smuggling. But here there was often a sort of tacit understanding between the authorities and the smugglers, a sort of cat-and-mouse game where each side knew what the other was up to, but they both tried to stay one step ahead of the game. Smuggling also seems to have attracted those with what today we would call an entrepreneurial spirit: brave, even foolhardy souls who enjoyed not only the material benefits brought by successful smuggling, but also the eternal battle to outwit the foe. Of course in Scotland the battle had an extra edge to it, as the anti-smuggling laws emanated from England and any course of action that would tweak the nose of the haughty English had to be a good thing.

Two of the greatest of all Scottish smugglers – but men known as much for their wit, daring and quickness of intelligence – were described by W.R. Mackintosh at the turn of the century in his book, *Around the Orkney Peat Fires* – a 'bannet', by the way, is a 'bonnet' or 'hat'.

A Great Talker

'James Smith was known as "Peedie Bannets". He resided in Stenness, and carried on smuggling in Stromness on Orkney. When driving his grey mare on the road, if he happened to meet a gauger – a revenue man – he never failed to present his snuff-box, and then began to tell some funny anecdotes, of which he seemed to have an unlimited store. In this way he succeeded in interesting the gauger until his mare had passed on with the contraband. One morning, however, the sly gauger made a capture.

'Peedie Bannets, who was a man of resource, took down the reins, adjusted the bridle, and began to walk before the mare in the fashion common to his class then. While doing so he was so lively and jocose that he kept the gauger (elated as he was by the seizure he had made) laughing so loudly that he never missed the sound of the mare's feet, and when he looked around at the head of Hamliboe the animal had disappeared as well as the load.

'The following may be taken as a specimen of Peedie Bannets' conversational powers. Seated in a public house with a crony, a stoup or can in one hand, and the other resting on his knee (and inside the enormous piece of head gear from which he derived his name) he would say: "Deed, gossip, I pat Johnnie tae th' toon ae time an' I gaed him a pound, an' th' witless blockhead bought a grand hat mead oot o' dog hair, an' me auld breeks, an' paid eighteen shillings for hid; an' he only haed hid on twa or three times till hid was uiseless. If he haed only bought a bannet like me ane, hid wid only cost him tree shillin an' wad laisted him for years."

'This wonderful bonnet was very large, and of the kind worn by merchants in those days. It was so big that Peedie Bannets could lay the edge on his shoulder, as he always did, and pull it down to windward.'

In the same mould as Peedie is the remarkable Mansie Eunson, a man of sharp wit, devious practice and low cunning. However, W.R. Mackintosh clearly has a soft spot for the rogue, as one suspects he would have for any Scot able to outwit a figure of English author-ity – a 'flesher', by the way, is a butcher.

THE REMARKABLE MANSIE EUNSON

'Mansie Eunson, a Kirkwall smuggler, is well known to the present generation. He was flesher, beadle, and a successful smuggler. In addition to this he was a born character, brim-ful of pawky humour and resource, which extricated him from many a scrape.

'One day he was walking along the St Andrews road, when he met Mr Baikie, the laird of Tankerness. Mansie had with him a dog, which was much admired, the laird describing it as a perfect beauty. "No thanks to it," replied Mansie. "It's weel fed, weel housed, an' it's free o' debt, which is more than you or me can say, laird!"

'It seems that the laird had been due an account to Mansie, and this was the sly way the old flesher took to remind him of the debt. Mansie did a big smuggling business, but he was so clever in carrying the goods after they were landed that he could never be caught, though he had many narrow escapes.'

Mansie Keeps The Exciseman Laughing

'On one occasion the excise officers got a hint that a cargo of spirits had been landed in the East Mainland, and they were determined to keep a strict eye on Mansie's movements. They watched him going away with his cart one afternoon, and they patiently awaited his return. When the cart reached Kirkwall, however, it was empty. A hint of the danger had been conveyed to the old smuggler, and he coolly planted the gin in a ditch a short distance from the town, carrying it in after the excise officers had been deceived by the empty cart.

'The gaugers at last began to suspect this trick, and resolved to go out the Holm Road and meet Mansie some miles from town. The night chosen was a very dark one, and they concealed themselves behind a stone wall. At length they heard the rattle of a cart in the distance, and were on the alert. As the vehicle got into line with them, they pounced out upon poor Mansie, and there, sure enough, was some half-dozen small kegs of gin and brandy. The officers were elated with their successful capture; but Mansie took the thing very coolly.

'He slipped the reins of his horse over its head, and began to walk some distance in front, keeping the excisemen in roars of laughter as he recounted to them many of the best of his large stock of anecdotes. In this way time passed quickly, and when Mansie arrived opposite his own house at the head of the Clay Loan, he turned his horse inwards, as if to unyoke.

' "No, no, Mansie," said the chief officer of excise, "you must bring your cart and its contents down to our premises. Seeing you have carried the spirits so far, you will not grudge taking them that extra distance."

' "Spirits," said Mansie in well-feigned surprise, "whaur are they?" The officers went over to the cart to show the kegs to Mansie, but, alas, they were gone.

'It is needless to say that the excisemen used some very strong language when they discovered they had been outwitted by the wily old smuggler. Mansie, to prevent accidents, was always accompanied by some friends when he went out on a smuggling expedition; and, knowing these were close at hand when he was caught by the excisemen, he depended upon them noiselessly removing the kegs from the cart while he kept the gaugers in good humour with his funny stories. The means that were taken to circumvent the excisemen were thus simple; but they were also effective.'

Putting Right A Gizzened Barrel

'On another occasion Mansie had brought a little keg of spirits into town in broad daylight, and before he had time to get it hidden, he noticed an exciseman coming up the Clay Loan. Mansie, who was full of resource, lifted the keg and dropped it into the water barrel. When the exciseman arrived at the house, the old smuggler was busy throwing water into the barrel.

' "Well, Mansie," said the exciseman, "what is this that you are so busy about to-day?"

' "Oh," replied Mansie, "my barrel was gizzened, and I'm trying to get it put right wi' water from the well, as there's no appearance o' ony rain comin." Mansie kept so cool that the officer was completely taken in and passed on, though the old smuggler declared afterwards that he did fear that he was to be caught on that particular occasion.'

A Pulpitful Of Spirits

'Smuggling was carried on to such an extent, and with such bad effects upon the people, that the clergymen began to denounce the traffic. One Sunday Mansie's minister held forth on the iniquity of the trade, and declared that no Christian would take any part in it. When the service was over, some person asked Mansie what he thought of the sermon.

' "I think," answered Mansie, " that oor minister is no' very consistent, for at the very time he was preaching, he had six kegs o' as guid brandy under his pulpit as ever was smuggled!"

'This joke was much appreciated, for Mansie, being church officer, often hid his smuggled spirits under the floor of the pulpit, pretty confident that that would be one of the last places that the excisemen would think of searching. Mansie was fond of practical joking, especially if indulging in it would assist him in his illicit trade. One night he wanted to bring in a quantity of spirits from Deerness, but was anxious to make sure that the excisemen should be out of the way. He met a man whom he suspected to be in league with the gaugers, and told him in secret that he was to cross the Bridge of Wideford between twelve and one o'clock next morning with three horses laden with kegs. This news was conveyed to the excisemen, and they took up their position under the bridge, so as to make a capture.

At just about one o'clock Mansie made his appearance, but he was coming from, instead of to, the town, and the kegs which he carried were empty. When asked for an explanation of his strange behaviour, Mansie said he had got the spirits into the town by another road, that he thought it would be a pity to keep the excisemen out all night in the cold, and that he had therefore come out to tell them that their watch was in vain!'

Mansie Is Saved By His Scouts

'On another occasion the excisemen got a hint that Mansie was to convey a number of kegs from Holm, that he was to carry them in "caisies" slung over the backs of horses, and that he was to avoid the public road and cross the heather. The officers accordingly made up their minds they would circumvent the old smuggler and spread themselves over the moor in such a way that it was impossible he could escape if he came that way.

'Mansie, however, had his scouts, and these gave him "wittance" of the nice little scheme that had been laid to capture him. He therefore piloted his kegs into town by the public road, in the murk of night, leaving the gaugers to their cold and lonely bed among the heather. With "the skreigh o' day" the officers came to Mansie's house; but by that time the "grice" had been safely planted. The old smuggler was therefore in a kindly mood, and laid before the officers some of the Holland, which he had just smuggled, to cheer them after their cold night's vigil.

' "Grand gin," says one of the officers, "where did you get it?" His host did not enlighten him on this point, but very pertinently reminded him of the text that runs: "Eat such things as are set before you, asking no questions!" '

A Cargo Of Oats

'In the winter of 1827–28, a vessel was brought into Kirkwall harbour with a cargo of oats which had been somewhat damaged. Those in authority decided to throw the grain overboard because it was not worth the duty payable upon it. When they began operations, Mansie appeared on the scene. Having equipped himself with some fishing tackle, he went with his boat and cast his anchor a little to windward of where the grain was being thrown into the sea, and paid out the boat's line until he came right alongside of the vessel. Those in authority saw that Mansie was getting his boat filled with the oats, and ordered him away.

' "I cam oot tae fish, an' ye'll sink me boat if ye keep haevin' thae oots in her this way," was Mansie's cool reply. When his boat was well filled he went to the shore and secured his boat. Others contented themselves with gathering up the oats after they had been washed ashore. After the grain had been secured it was washed with fresh water and dried on kilns, some of it being made into meal and some sown as seed and cropped. For this kind of smuggling they were not fined.'

Mansie Is Hard-Pressed

'Once Mansie was very hard pressed at Holm. He was carrying a keg on his shoulders when some rangers saw him and gave pursuit. Striking off the road, he made straight for a farmhouse, with the excisemen close in pursuit. After a race of about half a mile, Mansie was captured, but the keg he was carrying was empty! The people at the farm, who had witnessed the chase, secured an empty keg, and when Mansie was passing through the close

The Onslaught of the Smugglers *by Louis Eugene Gabriel Isabbey*

which separated the house from the byre, they exchanged casks with him. Fortunately the exciseman took the view that Mansie had hoaxed them and made no search at the farmhouse where the gin had been dropped.'

Mansie Gives Up Churchgoing

'At length Mansie was taken before the Session for smuggling, and he lost his situation as beadle. He took this so much to heart that he gave up attending church. One day the minister met Mansie and said "Mansie, you never come to church now."

'"O, what a lie," retorted Mansie. "My wife is there every Sunday."

'"But that is not you," urged the minister.

'"Well," replied Mansie, "when I was married, the minister told me wife an' me that we wis one, an' if we are no' one, either you or the other minister has telt us a lie!"

'Mansie and Peedie were clearly a cut above the rest, but the smugglers didn't always have it their own way. The fact is that they were caught, as often as not, and merely hoped to make enough money from each successful run to pay the fines when they were hauled before the magistrate.'

THE LEGENDARY JAMES WALKER

Our final tale from over the border concerns the capture of one of Scotland's toughest and most infamous smugglers, the legendary James Walker. The story comes from *The Weekly Scotsman* for 30 October 1909:

'James Walker of the Clyde had earned a reputation second to none. He had long eluded the police – with spies and informers everywhere, Walker snapped his fingers at the law, until a fateful day in October 1821.

'Powerful and athletic, swift of foot and sure of hand, and never without weapons of reference, he swore he would never be taken alive. From Largs to Ayr his name was familiar to all interested in the game of "jink the gauger", and there was not a hiding place within a dozen miles of the shore with which he was not acquainted.

'Then one day he walked out to the point of Troon Harbour to take ships to Ireland on one of his smuggling expeditions. The vessel for some reason had been delayed in her departure and meanwhile a traitor gave information of Walker's whereabouts to the excisemen. Steps were immediately taken to secure him, and aware of his desperate character, the greatest caution and secrecy were observed. Supported by a force of dragoons, the local exciseman, Gunn, marched toward the promontory and posted a strong line of sentinels across the connecting isthmus with strict instructions to let no one pass on any pretext. This done, Gunn and his corporal advanced along the quay to where their man was seated, quite unconscious of the danger impending. Happening to glance round, he realised the position of affairs instantly, sprang to his feet, rushed swiftly past Gunn, sent the corporal sprawling on the pier, then relying on his extraordinary fleetness of foot, leaped on to the rocks and bounded away like a deer, exciseman and soldier panting furiously behind him. But for the sentries barring the shoreward path he would have escaped. Still increasing the distance between him and his pursuers, Walker was beginning to hope for escape when, at a narrow part of the rocks, he swerved seaward, plunged boldly into the water and swam rapidly towards a sloop lying nearby, where he knew he would be safe. Unluckily for him, the dragoon was a better swimmer and he was soon dragged from the water vowing dire revenge upon his captors. He was relieved of his pistol and ammo, placed in a cart in irons and carried over six miles of rough road to the old cells of Ayr. And that was the last we heard of him.'

A more modern approach to smuggling: at the customs office in London in 1935, two cats are on the payroll at 3d a day to detect smuggled foodstuffs

BIBLIOGRAPHY

A Free Apology on Behalf of Smugglers (1749)

A Gentleman of Chichester (1745)

A Plain Address to Smugglers (1833)

Archbold, J.F. *Recent Acts Relating to Poaching* (1830)

Banks, John *Reminiscences of Smugglers and Smuggling* (1873)

Benham, Hervey *Once Upon a Tide* (1955)

Bishop, George *Observations, Remarks and Means to Prevent Smuggling* (1783)

Black, Elizabeth *Gentlemen Go By* (1933)

Bottrell, W. *Traditions and Hearthside Stories of West Cornwall* (1870)

Bowditch, James *A Treatise for the Prevention of... Smuggling* (1836)

Bradley, A.G. *An Old Gate of England* (1918)

Bridges, George *A Whip for the Smugglers* (1742)

— *Plain Dealing* (1744)

Burke, Thomas *English Inns* (1945)

Carter, Captain Henry *Autobiography of a Cornish Smuggler* (1894)

Chatterton, E.K. *Kings Cutters and Smugglers* (1912)

Clark, K. *Many a Bloody Affray* (1968)

Cooke, W. *The Cragsmen* (1913)

Cooper, William *Smuggling in Sussex* (1858)

Coxhead, J.R.W. *Smuggling Days in Devon* (1956)

Creswick, P. *Smugglers of Barnard's Head* (1899)

Crockett, S.R. *Tales of our Coast* (1896)

Cross, A.L. *Eighteenth Century Documents Relating to Smuggling* (1928)

Defoe, Daniel *Journal of a Tour Through England and Wales* (1725)

Dutt, W.A. *The Norfolk and Suffolk Coast* (1909)

English, John *Reminiscences of Old Folkestone Smugglers* (1885)

Farjeon, J. J. *The Compleat Smuggler* (1938)

Forbes, Athol *The Romance of Smuggling* (1909)

Graham, Frank *Smuggling Inns* (1966)

Hall, James *Travels in Scotland* (1807)

Hamilton Jenkin, A.K. *Cornish Seafarers* (1932)

— *Cornwall and its People* (1970)

Harding, R. *Serious Cautions to all involved in... Smuggling* (1818)

BIBLIOGRAPHY

Harper, Charles *Inns of Old England* (1927)

— *The Smugglers* (1909)

Harrison, Herbert *The Last of the Free Traders* (1937)

Harvey, E.G. *History of Mullyen* (1875)

Holmes, T.V. *Notes on a Box Used in Smuggling* Transactions of the Cumberland and Westmorland Association (1891)

Howe, John *Smuggler: A Journal* (1827)

Janssen, S.T. *Smuggling Laid Open* (1763)

Lapthorne, W.H. *Smugglers' Broadstairs* (1970)

Larn, Richard and Carter, Clive *Cornish Shipwrecks* (1969)

MacDonald, Ian *Smuggling in the Highlands* (1914)

Mackintosh, W.R. *Around the Orkney Peat Fires* (1914)

Maxwell Wood, John *Smuggling in the Solway* (1908)

Methley, V.M. *Smuggling Days* (1930)

Moray, A. *Diary of a Rum Runner* (1929)

Newball, J. *A Scheme to Prevent the Running of Wool...* (1744)

Nicholls, F.F. *Honest Thieves* (1973)

Page, J.L. *The Coasts of Devon and Lundy* (1895)

Page, W. (ed) *Victoria History of Cornwall* (1906)

— *Victoria History of Sussex* (1905)

Payne, Leonard *Practical Smuggling and Other Stories* (1929)

Pelham, E. *Naval History of Great Britain* (1823)

Rattenbury, Jack *Memoirs of a Smuggler* (1837)

Ready, Oliver *Life and Sport on the Norfolk Broads* (1910)

Reyer, Guy de *A Nomad of the Sea* (1936)

Rogers, Charles *Social Life in Scotland* (1869)

Row, Fred *Essex Survivals* (1966)

Shore, H.N. *Old Fowey Days* (1907)

— *Smuggling Days and Smuggling Ways* (1892)

— *The Smugglers* (1923)

Short, Bernard *Smugglers of Poole and Bournemouth* (1969)

Smith, G.C. *The Scilly Isles* (1828)

Smuggling in Sussex Sussex Archaeological Collection Vol X

Some Considerations of the Present State of Scotland (1744)

Suffolk Chronicle (1810)

Thompson, Leonard *Smugglers of the Suffolk Coast* (1968)

Thomson, W. *The Smuggling Era in Scotland* (1910)

Verrill, A.H. *Smugglers and Smuggling* (1924)

Warner, Rev Richard *Literary Recollections* (1830)

Welcome, J. *Best Smuggling Stories* (1967)

Western, J.R. *English Militia in the Eighteenth Century* (1965)

White, Allen *Eighteenth Century Smuggling in Christchurch* (1973)

Williams, N. *Contraband Cargoes* (1959)

INDEX

Page numbers in *italics* indicate illustrations

INDEX